What people are saying ~~about Framework Leadership~~ . . .

"Leadership, at its heart, is not about flowcharts and hierarchy, but about influence. A leader may think alone, pray alone, dream alone, but, ultimately, a leader must build a team to move toward the dream that is just ahead of them. Dr. Ingle outlines a proven process to influence and activate your future."

—John Maxwell, #1 *New York Times* bestselling author

"In *Framework Leadership*, Dr. Kent Ingle utilizes his vast leadership experience to offer timely advice on how to develop one's inherent leadership talents, which leads not only to personal development but to teamwork that brings success and contentment. This is a valuable resource for the production of both public and private leadership qualities. May God bless this endeavor."

—Benjamin S. Carson Sr. MD, professor emeritus of neurosurgery, oncology, plastic surgery, and pediatrics, Johns Hopkins Medicine; president and CEO, American Business Collaborative, LLC

"Any leader who is committed to getting better needs a fresh and ongoing supply of ideas and insights. *Framework Leadership* is a needed resource and the kind of book that will remind, refocus, and reinvigorate you. Kent Ingle writes from real-world leadership experiences, and his ideas are terrific."

—Mark Sanborn, president, Sanborn & Associates, Inc.; author, *The Fred Factor* and *You Don*¹*t Need a Title to Be a Leader*

"One of the toughest lessons I've learned as a leader is that what got me to where I am may not get me to where I need to go next. In a world of constant change, leaders can't rely on old methods and expect to succeed. God wants to do a new thing in us and through us. *Framework Leadership* is a toolbox that will help you do just that. I'm grateful to my friend, Dr. Kent Ingle, for writing such a timely, timeless book."

—**Mark Batterson**, *New York Times* bestselling author of *The Circle Maker*, lead pastor of National Community Church, Washington, D. C.

"*Framework Leadership* is a proven process for breakthrough. Kent Ingle has been leading for years, so trust his experience, knowledge, and know-how. He's navigated and led rapid seasons of innovation and change in several organizations, leading them from slow decline to rapid success. Kent is a turnaround specialist, focused ultimately on creating transformational change in organizations and the leaders who lead them. Let him show you how."

—**Brad Lomenick**, former president, Catalyst; founder, BLINC; author, *The Catalyst Leader* and *H3 Leadership*

"Dr. Ingle's work on leadership is a needed contribution to the debate on the required transformation that our society needs to thrive in this century. This book is his testament to his own contribution on authenticity and change, during his tenure as president at SEU."

—**Dr. Mark Esposito**, professor of Business and Economics, Grenoble School of Management, Harvard University's Division of Continuing Education and IE Business School; bestselling author of *Business Ethics* and *Emotional Intelligence & Hospitality*

"Dr. Kent Ingle is living out his divine design and making a significant impact in our world today. His book will help you build, discover, and develop your personal framework to live out your calling with purpose and greatness. Learn from one of the great leaders of our day."

—**Dr. Todd Mullins**, senior pastor, Christ
Fellowship, West Palm Beach, FL

"Dr. Kent Ingle is a great leader with a quiet confidence that brings a calm and strength to all those around him. I have been a firsthand witness of the change and leadership that Kent has been able to orchestrate and it seemed as if he knew the outcomes in advance! In his new book *Framework Leadership*, he outlines the principles and practices of this change process and the important disciplines needed to be ready for it. Kent has taught on our divine design, and now gives incredible insight into capitalizing upon that design to make a greater difference in the world around us."

—**Rob Ketterling**, lead pastor, River Valley Church,
Minneapolis, MN; author of *Front-Row Leadership*

"I have worked with Dr. Ingle for many years, and for all those years he has consistently communicated the need for organizations and organizational leaders to take a framework approach to leadership. This book is a roadmap for leaders looking to make a lasting and positive change in their organizations."

—**Dr. Brian Carroll**, executive vice president,
Southeastern University

FRAMEWORK
LEADERSHIP

POSITION YOURSELF FOR
TRANSFORMATIONAL CHANGE

KENT INGLE

Collaboration and Developmental Editing: Ben Stroup
(www.benstroup.com)—Greenbrier, TN

Cover and interior design by Prodigy Pixel
(www.prodigypixel.com)

ISBN: 978-1-68067-195-7
Printed in the United States of America
20 19 18 17 • 1 2 3 4 5

CONTENTS

FOREWORD

T he love of what you do and want to accomplish must be greater than your fear of failure. That's the resolve you need if you want to create change—and it all starts with passion and vision.

You must love what you do, have a clear vision, and operate from a sense of purpose that is greater than yourself. The secret to life and the greatest success strategy of all is to love all of it and fear none of it.

But fear exists everywhere, and if you aren't careful, this will distract you from your best work. If you're distracted, others around you will be distracted as well. It's a spiraling effect that can leave you feeling paralyzed, out of sync, and unable to see a clear path to success.

Your love for what you do can drive you to overcome the fear that is holding you back. I believe this is especially true in legacy organizations where precedents were set decades ago, and it can feel almost disingenuous to suggest alternate paths. But when your purpose transcends your personal desires, you can inspire people to join you in your journey.

Great leaders organize people around a shared vision. More important, the mark of true leadership is when a leader's vision can inspire others to work together collaboratively and interdependently. This is much easier to talk about than to do. There are so many pitfalls along the way and so many competing agendas that it can seem impossible to accomplish.

But when it does happen, it's almost magical. You can try to create change through force of will and sheer determination, but that almost always results in failure and unmet expectations. You can't carry the world on your back. Instead, you must recognize that change begins with your ability to translate your energy, passion, and clarity for a better future to others in a way that invites them to be part of something special, specific, and significant.

This is why I believe in Dr. Kent Ingle and the timeliness of his message. He has grown, transformed, and multiplied every organization he has led. And he's done it again at Southeastern University. He loves what he does more than he fears failure.

What he writes in this book is not a theory but a proven process that has been refined over time. Dr. Ingle understands that culture drives expectations and beliefs about what's possible. Those expectations, in turn, drive behavior, which influences habits. And habits, ultimately, create the future. This is why his concept around framework leadership is so powerful, practical, and relevant. It's not your goals that will lead you to success but your commitment to the process.

This book will help you discover a predictable path to success through the discipline of activating your vision through the actions you take and the influence you have on the people you lead. I'm grateful to Dr. Ingle for his love of leadership, the clarity of his vision, his desire to invest in building great people and organizations, and his unwavering resolve to stay true to his faith and principles. What a legacy!

Remember, you have only one ride through life, so give it all you've got! And enjoy the ride!

—**Jon Gordon**, *Wall Street Journal* bestselling author of
The Energy Bus and *You Win in the Locker Room First*

INTRODUCTION

*The place God calls you to is the place where your
deep gladness and the world's deep hunger meet.*

—Frederick Buechner

C an I let you in on a really important piece of news? God
is up to something in our world. Not only that, but you
are a vital part of His plans.

Maybe, as you read these words, you're thinking, *I'm not so
sure. I don't really feel all that special; how could God be planning
to do anything important with me?*

Or, you might be thinking, *That all sounds great, but I wish
God would let me in on His plans. I just don't think I'm getting
much of anywhere with all that I feel I ought to be accomplishing.*

If you had either of those two reactions, or even if you
know someone who might have had either reaction, then I
want to offer you a special invitation to keep reading. In these
pages, I'm going to share with you why I believe so strongly
that you—yes, you!—have a great purpose in life. Not only that,
but I believe just as strongly that you can help other people
find and align with their purposes in life in order to accomplish
amazing things that will make the world a better place and that
will cause it to become more of what God meant for it to be.

I'm convinced that there is a divine design for your life, and that by pursuing that design—and even by helping others to do the same—you can fulfill the destiny God has been planning for you since the creation of the universe.

Are you interested in hearing more? Good!

Designed for a Purpose

Your DNA was crafted by God. Let that idea soak in for a moment. Stamped on every cell of your being is the imprint of the Master Creator. I know this is true, because the Bible says that God "created my inmost being" and that He "knit me together in my mother's womb" (Ps. 139:13). Could this possibly be expressed any more intimately? God wove you together, as a skilled weaver creates a beautiful, complex tapestry on a loom. The Bible also assures us that we are made in the image of God; we carry His likeness within us. I promise you, there is no higher pedigree than that.

What this means is that you matter—in fact, you matter infinitely. God made you for a unique purpose. Not only that, but as you have gone through your life, God has placed opportunities in your path so that you will have a chance to begin to fulfill that purpose. Even when you don't take maximum advantage of these opportunities—or even when, sometimes, you miss them altogether—you are walking a path through life that is designed to provide you, time and again, with those divine appointments that reveal the doorway to your purpose in life.

God has also placed within your heart and mind a passion to pursue that purpose. Whether you realize it or not, you carry within you a longing to accomplish something that makes a difference in your family, your community, or the world. I love the way that writer and minister Frederick Buechner expresses this in the quote that opens this introduction.[1] And it's true! In those times when you are most intently utilizing your passion to make a difference, you will find that you are also most deeply content. It just makes sense: When we're doing what we were designed to do, we're at our best and are most satisfied.

Finally, you haven't gotten as far as you have in life without having acquired a certain amount of discipline. After all, if you can read this book and understand the words, you have demonstrated the discipline of learning to read. And if you're enrolled in a class or working a job, that means that, at least most of the time, you have the discipline to show up at the necessary time and place to continue your participation. I'm sure there are times when you wish you had more discipline— we all do! I'm writing these words a couple of days after the Thanksgiving holiday. I wish I'd had a little more discipline to push back sooner from the table. No doubt, there are areas of your life where you wish you could exhibit a stronger sense of discipline. But the point is, that discipline—in whatever quantity—is a tool God has placed within you to enable you to arrive at those points of opportunity where your passion meets the world's greatest needs. When you have developed your discipline so that it carries you to the place where your passion intersects with the divine opportunities in your path, you are poised to transform your life and the lives of others.

The Courage to Commit

Passion and discipline, as important as they are, can only carry you so far. You must also exercise the conviction and courage to act on what you believe about yourself. When passion and discipline bring you to the brink of your next divine opportunity, you still need the courage to take the next step. There are times when that step may seem like walking off the end of a diving board in the dark. Yet, it is only through such acts of courage and conviction that potential is translated into reality. When your next step involves inviting others to share your vision—to join you in pursuing the opportunity God is calling you to accept—conviction is absolutely essential. The fact is that people don't follow leaders who are halfhearted or tentative. On the other hand, when courage and conviction are wedded with passion and the discipline to pursue the divine opportunity, people with willing hearts will flock to the cause. A quote often attributed to John Wesley says it this way: "Light yourself on fire with passion and people will come from miles around to watch you burn."

Breakthrough Leadership

If you look at some of the most important movements in history, you'll find they all have one important factor in common: None of them happened just because a leader had a great idea; they happened because a leader had a great idea and was able to inspire others to do something significant, special, and meaningful. It may be true, as the adage says, that nothing is more powerful than an idea whose time has come, but I suggest that what gives the idea its power is the ability of a visionary leader to motivate the hearts, minds, and imaginations of others—to unite people under a cause greater than any single person. Great leaders have great ideas, but they are also able to give those ideas an articulate tongue, tireless legs and feet, strong arms and hands.

At first glance, Dan Phillips doesn't appear like someone who could ignite a movement. A former rodeo cowboy, military intelligence officer, and dance instructor, the wiry, ponytailed seventy-year-old looks like someone who would be more comfortable in the cab of a pickup than onstage in front of a live audience. Yet, his TED Talk, delivered October 6, 2010, brought to an international audience Dan's innovative vision for sustainable, affordable low-income housing.[2] Dan and his for-profit company, Phoenix Commotion, build using reclaimed and recycled materials, which reduces the landfill burden. They also employ unskilled laborers—including the prospective homeowners—thus providing training in marketable skills and reducing the cost of construction. All of Dan's homes are built to code and approved by qualified electricians, engineers, and plumbers.

Ask people in Dan's hometown of Huntsville, Texas, about what he's doing, and you'll likely get a raving fan's-eye view of the importance of sustainably built housing. You might even get a tour of one of the unique homes, built and trimmed out with materials like license plates, non-standard sized pieces of plywood, fragments of shattered mirrors, mismatched bricks, bottle caps, or—as in the case of perhaps Dan's most famous creation—animal bones. Phoenix Commotion and Dan, who is fond of advocating escape from "the tyranny of the two-by-four and the four-by-eight," have been featured in news stories and documentaries appearing in Oprah.com, *People*, the *New York Times*, the *Today Show*, Ireland's *Eco E-Zine*, the Associated French Press, and the Beijing News.[3]

But if you ask Dan what motivates him, he'll tell you that it all started with an idea: It was possible to solve at once both the problem of affordable housing for low-income families and the problem of adverse environmental impacts by the traditional building industry. In a March, 2002, interview, he said, "In a town [the size of Huntsville], about 30,000 people, we throw away enough material to build a house every week. When we have families who can't afford a home, that's the height of arrogance."[4] Once Dan had that idea and began acting on his convictions, others started to notice—and to join his movement. The result is that since mortgaging his home to establish Phoenix Commotion in 1997, Dan has helped dozens of families move into houses of their own that they helped build for themselves. In the process, he has given on-the-job training "to anyone with a work ethic who is willing to swing a hammer," and has inspired a small army of enthusiasts to think greener, to get creative, and to make maximum use of what they have on hand.

What separates people like Dan Phillips from those who don't see their dreams through to completion? I believe it comes down to being aware of their driving passion, seeing the divine opportunities in their path, and having the courage to act. Like Dan Phillips, breakthrough leaders are, above all, aware of the context—both internal and external—in which they are acting. Leaders with these critical attributes and this crucial awareness are able, like Dan Phillips, to take what is available and craft it into the reality of their passion. They are able to assemble a framework that stabilizes, clarifies, enables, and actualizes the divine design of both the leader and the followers.

Framework Leadership

In this book, I want to help you not only to discover and develop your divine design, but also to sensitize you to the context in which you are seeking to create meaningful change. I want to help you recognize the characteristics necessary for both personal and organizational change. I believe the reason some leaders can successfully communicate the vision in a way that motivates and inspires—and others can't—comes down to the ability to envision and foster a framework: a context for bringing a vision into reality. With the right kind of framework in place, people and organizations not only survive disappointment and failure, they transform them into fuel for ultimate success. The proper framework empowers people and groups to advance their mission, even while overcoming difficulty or adapting to internal and external change.

When you act within the proper framework, you can multiply your vision in the lives of those on your team. You will see the breakthrough before it happens and will be able to communicate it effectively and convincingly. You will be able to forge your team into a cohesive unit that celebrates each member's unique talents while still driving toward a single goal. You will be able to perceive when adjustment—or even major realignment—is needed, and communicate that in a way that energizes, rather than intimidates. You will be able to assess what is available—both in resources and in talent—and adopt the best strategy for putting it to use. The proper framework can make people and organizations almost infinitely adaptable, while still remaining true to the mission and focused on success.

You are created for greatness, intended to live with passion, discipline, and courage. With framework leadership, you will be able to share yourself most effectively with others. And you will help them to discover the greatness within themselves.

CHAPTER ONE

Framework Leadership

"I have never been lost, but I was once mighty turned around for three days."[5]

—Daniel Boone

H ave you ever considered the importance of knowing where you are? For example, when you're in an unfamiliar shopping mall and you're trying to find a particular store, what do you look for? If you're like me, you try to find one of those signs with a schematic layout of the place featuring a brightly colored dot labeled "You are here."

If you know where you are, you can usually figure out how to get wherever you want to go. But if you can't locate where you are, then all you can do is wander aimlessly, hoping you'll see something that looks familiar.

This is one of the fundamental principles of framework leadership: You must know the context in which you are operating—you've got to know where you are. You've got to know the people, the circumstances, the resources, the challenges, the limitations, the goals, the history, the competition. You've got to know everything you can about the situation, and then you've got to have a clear vision for where you want to go in order to go from "you are here" to "you are where you want to be."

Paralysis from Lack of Analysis

We all know the old tennis player's trick, right? She asks you, very casually, as you're getting ready to play a match, exactly where you position your thumb as you're preparing your backhand stroke. Naturally, you've never really thought about that in such specific terms; you just hit the shot. But now, walking toward the baseline, you're puzzling over your opponent's seemingly innocent question. And for the rest of the match, your backhand goes AWOL. Why? Because you're analyzing your grip instead of hitting the stroke. Golfers often suffer from the same affliction; it's called "paralysis from analysis."

Clearly, there's a time for action—for just doing it. But I have to tell you, when leaders fail, it's often because of the opposite problem. Ignoring the context, or lacking an adequate grasp of it, they confidently march off in one direction or another, expecting others to fall into line. The trouble is, when we attempt to lead others—or even to just direct ourselves—without a clear understanding of the context and its implications for the undertaking, we usually end up confused and even paralyzed by uncertainty. I'm convinced that the biggest mistake leaders make is to act without adequate planning and especially without having a framework for success that is based on the context. Rather than too much analysis, leaders who fail have often neglected to analyze and understand exactly where they are.

The Framework Is Vital

In order for leadership to work—whether corporate, religious, civic, political, or even personal—it must be situated in a conceptual framework that embraces both the context and the intended outcome. Leaders must have clarity of vision about where they are and where they intend to take the enterprise. Not only that, but they must have an awareness of the resources—human and otherwise—and processes needed to negotiate the distance between present circumstances and realization of the vision.

The framework, if properly assembled, encompasses the environment in which the leader's vision becomes reality. It provides clarity, direction, purpose, and even method to navigate toward a new reality.

It's important to remember that the elements of the framework can and should be different for each leader and each context. Certainly, there are many qualities and attributes that great leaders share, but each person and situation is different and displays its own particular attributes.

For Alexander the Great, the central framework principle was common purpose. This military and political genius carried Greek culture and civilization across the entire known world of his day. Over his twelve-year campaign of conquest, from roughly 335 to 323 BC, he and his soldiers covered some 22,000 miles of territory that included 15,000-foot peaks and vast stretches of arid country. He defeated armies that outnumbered his forces, sometimes by four or five times. He was able to do these things because he was immensely successful at forging together his Hellenistic followers in pursuit of a unifying ideal: binding the world together with the tenets of Greek philosophy and culture.

Steve Jobs, on the other hand, built his leadership framework around a single word: *innovation*. Certainly, as we now know, he could be dictatorial, impatient, and even ruthless at times. But those who followed him knew that he possessed a quality of vision that was almost uncanny in its accuracy when it came to anticipating trends and how to capitalize on them. In his pursuit of the ideal technological solutions to the problems faced by consumers, Jobs was able to formulate alternatives that no one had previously considered. He was then able to persuade, cajole, and occasionally browbeat others into joining with him to make innovation a reality. Recent technological development has validated, over and over, the accuracy of Jobs' foresight.

For Thomas Edison, the key framework element was determination. He is famous for his answer to an associate who asked if he wasn't discouraged that he hadn't gotten any results despite performing scores of experiments: "I have gotten a lot of results! I know several thousand things that won't work." He also said, "Many of life's failures are people who didn't realize how close they were to success when they gave up."[6] Through such determination, Edison developed not only the inventions represented by the 1,093 US patents held in his name, but also the process of mass production that permitted his inventions to become part of everyday life for many people of the world. Our modern telecommunications, power generation, sound recording, and motion picture industries, in particular, probably wouldn't exist but for Edison and his legendary ethic of determination.

> Whatever your core motivation is, it is probably the principal raw material for your framework.

What is your guiding principle? What is the attribute that means the most to you as you pursue your dream? Are you doggedly determined, like Thomas Edison—one who refuses to quit until the goal is reached? Do you have the ability to innovate as Steve Jobs did, to think in new ways about the problems people face or how they can more quickly achieve their aspirations? Or do you have, like Alexander the Great, the ability to unify people in order to achieve a common goal? Are you able to build and motivate teams in order to accomplish something no one previously imagined could be done?

Your essential framework quality could be one of these, or it could be something completely different. But whatever your core motivation is, it is probably the principal raw material for your framework As you conduct a careful self-inventory of your special abilities, interests, dreams, passions, and especially the divine opportunities that have brought you along the path to where you are today, watch for the unifying trends that can give you insights about your framework for leadership. And then, once you've found it, find ways to build everything you do around it. In this way, your efforts will proceed from your most authentic self. You won't be playing a role; you'll be engaging yourself and others in the most honest way possible.

Of course, just reaching the point described above assumes that you have a certain level of self-awareness. It assumes that you have disciplined yourself to be alert for those quiet promptings, chance conversations, or inner aspirations that have aimed you in the direction that your passion is driving you. In short, evaluating and becoming aware of your leadership framework requires that you have already sensitized yourself to God's divine calling. It further requires that you have exercised or are developing the disciplines that will enable you to effectively share your vision with others.

Framework and Context

If you take a single principle away from this book, make it this: To be effective, the leadership framework must not only take into consideration the context; it must arise from and be integrated into it. Effective leadership isn't a one-size-fits-all quality. The history of business, in particular, is densely populated with stories of leaders who were phenomenally successful in one context but failed in another. When leaders don't assemble their leadership framework with adequate attention to the context—personal, financial, spiritual, relational, competitive—the framework will break down, and the leadership effort will fail.

Take, for example, Bob Nardelli. In the 1970s, he went to work for General Electric and soon became a rising star in the company. Jack Welch, the legendary CEO of GE, was his idol and mentor, and Nardelli had his eye fixed on the CEO position, following Welch's retirement. But the job of succeeding Welch went to someone else, and Nardelli quickly accepted an offer to become CEO of Home Depot.

However, the context at Home Depot was completely different than at GE. The autocratic, top-down, centralized philosophy that served GE so well under Jack Welch did not sit well at Home Depot, where individual knowledge, innovation, and initiative were highly prized. In 2007, after seven years of intermittent conflict with shareholders and employees, Nardelli was ousted as CEO. Sadly, in 2009, Nardelli, though undoubtedly a talented and dedicated leader, was named by *Condé Nast Portfolio* as "One of the Worst American CEOs of All Time."[7]

Effective leadership isn't a one-size-fits-all quality.

Nardelli's framework for leadership at Home Depot failed to take into consideration the changed context in which he was operating. Because of that, his efforts were, more often than not, at cross-purposes with the dominant ethic and values of the people at Home Depot. It's important to note, also, that Home Depot didn't crater under his leadership. The stock value held steady; the company instituted many cost-cutting and efficiency measures that benefited the bottom line. The problem is that during the same time period, Home Depot's principle competitor, Lowe's, doubled its stock price and gained market share over Home Depot. Nardelli didn't fail—not exactly—but the friction and inefficiencies caused by his lack of attention to context in his leadership framework caused the company to lose ground in the marketplace. It also led to his eventual ouster.

On the other hand, Lord Admiral Horatio Nelson was victorious in one of the most decisive naval engagements in history, precisely because of his awareness of context and the way he used it to construct the leadership framework. Prior to the Battle of Trafalgar, Nelson carefully placed those who would command the vessels in his fleet. He briefed them painstakingly on the plan for the battle and on what they should do as conditions evolved. He gave them exhaustive information on the circumstances they were likely to face and on how they should respond in various scenarios.

This intense preparation, based on Nelson's knowledge of the context, proved to be the deciding factor in the engagement—especially since Nelson was mortally wounded when the battle started. Though he didn't live long enough to see the results of his leadership, the English navy defeated a superior force, sinking or incapacitating twenty-two enemy ships without losing a single vessel. Nelson's framework for leadership empowered his commanders—with the result that they were able to succeed even when he was no longer able to coordinate their efforts personally.

In the Bible, we find this framework leadership principle at work. For example, early in the life of the church, the founding apostles faced a challenge arising from the context. In Acts 6, we read that there was a problem between the Jewish believers who spoke Greek and were likely from other parts of the Roman Empire, and those who spoke Aramaic and were from the area surrounding Jerusalem. The widows, who depended on the church's daily distributions of food in order to survive, were being treated unequally. The Aramaic-speaking widows ("the native Hebrews," as Acts calls them) were being taken care of much better than the Greek-speaking widows.

When the problem was brought to the apostles, they made a wise decision. They asked the church to find seven dependable people who could oversee the food distribution and make sure it was done fairly. We read in Acts 6:5–6, "This proposal pleased the whole group. They chose Stephen, a man full of faith and of the Holy Spirit; also Philip, Procorus, Nicanor, Timon, Parmenas, and Nicolas from Antioch, a convert to Judaism. They presented these men to the apostles, who prayed and laid their hands on them." And the result of this delegation of duties? The next verse says, "So the word of God spread. The number of disciples in Jerusalem increased rapidly, and a large number of priests became obedient to the faith" (Acts 6:7).

For the apostles, the essential framework element was their own dedication to prayer and the leadership of the Holy Spirit. Working from that context, they developed the leadership strategy needed to address the challenges in the context and allow the enterprise (the infant church) to move forward successfully.

Building Your Own Framework

By now, I hope you have a healthy respect for the importance of the leadership framework to empowered and effective leadership. As you begin the journey of bringing the vision God has placed within you to reality, I believe it's absolutely vital for you to assemble your framework to encompass all the factors in your context.

One of the most important tools you have at your disposal is your ability to listen. In fact, listening is the essential first step in effective communication. And, as we all know, communication is central to understanding. So, in the next chapter, let's take the next step toward understanding the leadership framework by considering how great leaders are, first and foremost, great listeners.

CHAPTER ONE IN REVIEW

• Before you can know how to reach your destination, you need to know where you are right now and where you want to go.

• You can't lead effectively without a thorough understanding of the context.

• The context includes the people, resources, and circumstances necessary for success. It also includes the challenges, competition, and limitations you must overcome.

• The leadership framework arises out of the context.

• Your guiding attribute is the key to constructing your leadership framework.

QUESTIONS FOR DISCUSSION

1. Do you have a clear idea of where you are right now, in comparison with where you want to be?

2. What is your principal motivational attribute or core ethical principle? If there were a single quality you could be known for, what would it be?

3. As you think about reaching your goals, what resources are available to you to get started? Who are the people you need to have around you in order to be successful? What competitive or other challenges will you face?

CHAPTER TWO

Listening Actively, Leading Attentively

To listen is an effort; just to hear is no merit. A duck hears, also.

—Igor Stravinsky

I f your high school experience was anything like mine, you probably had an awkward conversation with one or more of your teachers that started something like this:

Teacher: Are you listening? (Usually asked after a long pause when you suddenly realize you've been asked a question.)

Student: Yes, I heard you.

Teacher: You may have heard me, but are you *listening*?

There's a big difference between hearing and listening, isn't there? Igor Stravinsky, the great Russian composer of *The Rite of Spring* and other masterpieces of the early twentieth century, knew this very well.[8] Simply to hear—to perceive vibrations in the air with the auditory apparatus—is not the same thing as listening. Listening requires understanding—it requires engagement. To be a really good listener, you must be active—you must participate.

Listening Is Not a Spectator Sport

Most of us have taken a speech course in either high school or college, and the training we received in these classes is great. Being able to get up in front of a group and express yourself clearly and in an organized manner is a crucial life skill. But I have to admit, I sometimes wonder why more schools don't offer a listening course. After all, it doesn't matter how eloquent or well-organized you are as a speaker if no one is listening to what you say. I maintain that being a really good, really skilled listener is at least as important in leadership as being a skilled speaker. In fact, listening may be even more important! And the key to listening well is being an active listener.

Now, I'm not necessarily talking about the techniques that salespeople are sometimes taught: learning how to prompt someone who is speaking in such a way that their words give you an opening to present your product or idea. That, in my mind, isn't active listening; that's just waiting for your chance to say what you've already decided to say.

Instead, I believe that active listening involves really hearing what your conversation partner is saying—even what he or she *isn't* saying. It is hearing not just the words, but the emotions, the concerns, the experiences, and the beliefs behind the words. And the only way to do that is to participate— to be intentional as a

A listener who is truly engaged and intentional is working really hard.

listener. You must listen with the goal of understanding, of empathizing, of truly seeing the conversation from the other person's point of view.

This is especially difficult when we are communicating with someone with whom we are in disagreement. All too often in such a situation, our "listening" becomes nothing more than the interval between our rebuttals. If we do actually listen to what the other is saying, it's sometimes only so we can catch them in a mistake or an unsupported statement that we can use to win a point in the argument.

Certainly, in leadership situations, there will be times when we must express disagreement, occasions when we must make a decision that goes against someone's wishes. But the great leaders are those who, when making those tough calls, have already listened carefully, empathetically, and actively to every point of view—even the ones they may disagree with or decide not to implement. That type of listening is tough; it takes a lot out of you! It requires really digging deep into what the other person is saying and allowing that person's thoughts, opinions, and beliefs to enter your mind and heart—even to cause you to question your own views.

When seen in this way, it becomes clear that "active listening" is anything but an oxymoron! A listener who is truly engaged and intentional is working really hard. And it is that type of arduous, self-denying attentiveness that sets the exceptional leaders apart from those who are merely "in charge."

The Power of Positive Listening

You may have heard the story about the spouse who was attending a party with his wife where he would meet her coworkers for the first time. He really wanted to make a good impression, and as the date for the party drew near, he realized his stress level was going through the roof. He was extremely nervous about saying or doing the wrong thing and making things at work more difficult for his wife.

On the way to the party, he hit upon a plan: he would do nothing but listen to what others said to him and reflect back to them what they had said. So, when they walked into the party and he was introduced to someone, he would maintain eye contact with that person, nodding as they spoke, and responding, when necessary, with phrases like "I understand. You feel it's important that . . . " All evening long he did this; he avoided expressing any of his own opinions, and he carefully listened and accurately repeated back what he heard the other person say.

In the car on the way home, his wife informed him that he was the hit of the party. "Everyone was talking about what a great guy you were, how articulate you were—a couple of them even said you were downright charismatic."

Of course, he had barely spoken the whole night except to repeat back what he had heard someone just say! Yet, in the opinion of the partygoers, he was the most interesting conversation partner in the whole place.[9]

The moral is obvious, isn't it? One of the most powerful ways you can impact another person is to sincerely, intently, and carefully listen to what the person is saying to you. In fact, being known as a good listener can give you the type of influence over others that you can get in no other way. The fact is that every human being on the planet longs, more than anything else, to be truly understood. If you're a skilled, intentional, and active listener, you can offer to almost everyone you meet the thing everyone craves the most. In return, those to whom you give this precious gift will grant you their time, their appreciation, and—crucial for those in leadership—their trust.

> If you're a skilled, intentional, and active listener, you can offer to almost everyone you meet the thing everyone craves the most.

If you want to be the type of leader who earns and retains the confidence of a team; who has an accurate understanding of the team's capabilities and challenges; who can cast a vision that embraces everyone in the enterprise; then you need to develop and hone your skills of active listening.

On the other hand, failing to listen well can lead to tragedy. In fact, one of the most fateful events in the history of the nation of Israel was the direct result of the failure of a leader to listen well. In 1 Kings 12 we read the story of Rehoboam, the son of the great and wise King Solomon, when Rehoboan went up to the city of Shechem to receive the loyalty oaths of the people and leaders in the northern part of his kingdom.

Rehoboam was inheriting one of the greatest and most powerful kingdoms in the Mediterranean world at that time. His grandfather, King David, and his father, King Solomon, had between them subdued most of the surrounding nations. Solomon had extended trade far and wide, bringing the riches of nations into Jerusalem. His wisdom and the glory of his reign became legendary during his own lifetime, so that monarchs from as far away as southern Arabia journeyed to Jerusalem to see if the stories were true (1 Kings 10:2).

Yet not everyone in Israel had good thoughts about King Solomon. When Rehoboam arrived in Shechem, a delegation of leading citizens met with him and said, "Your father put a heavy yoke on us, but now lighten the harsh labor and the heavy yoke he put on us, and we will serve you" (1 Kings 12:4). Rehoboam asked for some time to consider the request, and he asked the opinions of two groups of advisors: the older, more experienced men who had served his father, and a group of younger men closer to his own age.

The older counselors advised Rehoboam to agree to the people's request: "If today you will be a servant to these people and serve them and give them a favorable answer, they will always be your servants" (1 Kings 12:7). But the younger courtiers advised Rehoboam, ". . . tell them, 'My little finger is thicker than my father's waist. My father laid on you a heavy yoke; I will make it even heavier. My father scourged you with whips; I will scourge you with scorpions'" (1 Kings 12:10–11).

Tragically, Rehoboam gave in to his ego and rejected the

advice given by the older men. He announced to his northern subjects his intention to be even harsher than his father had been. The immediate result was a rebellion that split the kingdom of Israel in two. The rest of Old Testament history is a sad tale of the gradual descent into servitude and bondage of both halves of this once-mighty kingdom. The eventual devastation of both the northern and southern portions of Israel resulted directly from Rehoboam's failure to listen carefully to the right people.

Listening When Everybody Else Wants You to Talk

As I look back on my own career—so far, at least—I think the time that the power of listening was most apparent was when I interviewed for the post of president at Southeastern University. Bear in mind: I was the outsider from the West Coast, coming to a school in Florida that had been led for decades by a beloved president who had only recently stepped down.

On the day of my principle interviews with faculty, directors, and other vital stakeholders, the agenda began at 7:00 in the morning and didn't finish until 9:00 p.m. This was their opportunity to evaluate me as a potential leader; without doubt, their decision on hiring me would hinge on the impressions they took away from our conversations. It was, to say the least, an important day.

It might not surprise you to learn that one of the questions I got that day—over and over, in every interview—was, "What is your vision for Southeastern University?" What might surprise you was my answer: "I don't know."

Before you conclude that either I'm not very bright or that I didn't really want the job, consider what I said next: "I can't tell you my vision, because I don't know you. Until I understand the potential of the people, I can't possibly envision the potential of the organization."

What I was trying to help them understand was that until I

had listened—carefully, painstakingly, and thoroughly—to the faculty, the students, the directors, the community, and all the other stakeholders so vital to the future and the direction of Southeastern University, I wouldn't be able to formulate a plan, a strategy, or a vision. And, when you think about it, to attempt to enunciate any vision I might have had for the school without doing the requisite listening would have been egotistical and, likely, disastrous.

Was there pressure on me to impress my listeners with my grand strategies for leading Southeastern into the future? Sure. After all, the reason they had me there in the first place was to evaluate me as a potential leader for the institution. They had not only the right, but the responsibility, to be curious about where I thought I might take them. But until I knew as much as I could reasonably learn about the people I would be working with, how could I know what we would be able to accomplish?

> Great leaders listen—actively, carefully, and completely.

Now, to be clear, I wasn't saying something like, "Oh, gee, I don't know; let me talk to a few people and get back to you on that." I was very intentional that formulating a logical and coherent leadership strategy was Job #1. But I was just as clear that until I had done my job as a listener, I couldn't decide how to shape my role as a leader. Fortunately for me, I have been blessed at Southeastern with a phenomenal leadership team and amazing support from the community, and our results the past few years will bear that out. But until I knew them and understood the context in which I would be leading, I wasn't ready to announce the directions we would be taking together.

Of course, this wasn't my first time to realize the primacy of listening to meaningful leadership. As a young sportscaster on the West Coast, I talked to my friends and acquaintances to find out what they liked and didn't like in a sports broadcast. One of the things I heard consistently was, "It would be really nice to be able to see the scores of other games while watching the broadcast." I heard this so much that I decided to see what could be done about it. Fortunately, I had a producer at the station who was willing to take a chance on something that hadn't been attempted—in our area, at least—and I became the first sports broadcaster in my part of California to have scores from other athletic contests scrolling across the bottom of the screen during the show. By listening to what our viewers were telling us, we were able to take a huge leap forward, competitively.

Similarly, when I assumed the leadership of a church in Thousand Oaks, where I served for a number of years, we started by listening—to the members, the people living in the neighborhood around the church, and others. Ultimately, as the leadership team gained a clearer and more defined picture of the needs of the church and community, we concluded that the best strategy for continued growth and relevance was to relocate the building, rename the church, and build an entirely new ministry program, geared to the needs, issues, and values we had discovered from listening.

I don't think I can say it strongly enough: Great leaders listen—actively, carefully, and completely.

Active Listening and Framework Leadership

When you, as a leader, practice active listening, you're not only building trust, confidence, and shared vision among your team members, you're also utilizing your most powerful means of acquiring all the necessary information about the leadership context. By listening actively, you gain access to the cues—both overt and implied—biases, feedback, concerns, priorities, values, abilities, and constraints of your team. More importantly, you obtain these assets by means more accurate and efficient than any survey, questionnaire, or focus group

By attending carefully and intentionally to the honest expression of your team's thoughts, beliefs, concerns, and values, you are equipping yourself with the crucial intelligence you need to assess the context for your leadership framework. After all, what could be more important contextually than the genuine emotional, intellectual, and ethical makeup of your team? These are the people on whom you will depend to execute the leadership vision that you articulate. By listening to them actively, intently, and carefully, you afford yourself the all-important leadership advantage of accurate knowledge. By actively listening, you obtain one of the most crucial tools for building your leadership framework strategy.

CHAPTER TWO IN REVIEW

• Hearing isn't the same as listening; it's more intentional and focused.

• Active listening requires involvement and effort.

• Being a good listener is at least as important as being a good speaker.

• Great leaders are almost always great listeners.

• People are profoundly influenced by those who listen actively to them; they're also profoundly alienated by those who refuse to listen well.

• Active, intentional listening is a crucial tool for framework leadership.

QUESTIONS FOR DISCUSSION

1. Think of the last time someone really listened to you. How did it make you feel?

2. What is your main challenge when listening to someone else? Does your mind wander? Do you start thinking of what you want to say? Do you have a hard time keeping your opinions to yourself?

3. How important is eye contact for active listening? Why do you think this is the case?

4. Why do you think it's hard to listen to people with whom you disagree? How might listening to them lead to a solution?

CHAPTER THREE

The Contextual Audit

Knowledge is knowing a tomato is a fruit;
wisdom is not putting it in a fruit salad.

—Miles Kington

C ontext is really important, isn't it? I love the quote above by Miles Kington,[10] because it illustrates this unforgettably. A slice of fresh, garden-grown tomato, laid across a hamburger patty still sizzling from the grill or chopped into a crisp, green salad—these are images that can make almost anyone salivate. But imagine that same tomato diced up and in a bowl with bananas, apples, cherries, and oranges . . . ugh! Not a combination of tastes I'd ever experience voluntarily. As Guy Clark famously sang, there aren't too many things better than homegrown tomatoes, but only if they are presented in the proper context.

It's true in the world of sports, too. When you hear the word "strike" in baseball, it means that a batter is a bit closer to walking away from the plate unsuccessful. But when a bowler yells, "Strike!" it means he or she has just achieved the best possible result in a single roll of the ball. It's all about context.

A friend of mine told me about a church youth group that went down to Mexico for a summer mission trip. They were helping a local congregation construct a church building, and plenty of sweaty, back-breaking labor was involved.

The group included both girls and guys, and of course the kids packed for the trip, knowing it was going to be hot in Mexico in the middle of the summer. Many of the girls wore the type of clothing they would have worn inw their own neighborhoods in hot weather: shorts, tank tops, and sandals or flip-flops. In other words, they looked like typical American teenage girls; back home, their attire probably wouldn't have drawn a second glance.

But they failed to take the cultural context of Mexico into account. In Mexico, despite the heat, proper women and girls don't typically show as much skin as American girls tend to do in the summer. As a result, when the young women from the youth group went to the store or walked from the job site to their hotel, they drew a type of attention from the local men that made them very uncomfortable. Wisely, one of the women sponsors for the group, familiar with this aspect of the Mexican cultural context, had brought some extra changes of loose-fitting shirts and pants for the girls to put on. After a day or two of being openly gawked at and hearing wolf-whistles and suggestive comments

> **Skilled leaders familiarize themselves with the context almost to the point of obsession, absorbing everything they can in order to completely understand the environment in which they are operating.**

when they were out in public, the American girls were only too happy to adjust their attire to the context.

Context drives and transforms meaning. For leaders, context is also the fuel, the raw material of the leadership framework. Skilled leaders learn how to read the context in order to discern the capabilities of a team member, the challenges presented by a change in situation, or the implications of a strategy. Unlike the somewhat naïve girls in the church youth group, skilled leaders familiarize themselves with the context almost to the point of obsession, absorbing everything they can in order to completely understand the environment in which they are operating. They know that divorced from the context the leadership framework will be flawed, ill-fitting, and ultimately doomed to fail.

Context Is Objective

Certain aspects of the leadership context are easy to deduce: the financials, the competition, the economics, the infrastructure. These are the contextual elements that often yield most easily to the leader's analysis. Objective context usually involves the more concrete dimensions of the environment—the types of things you imagine that you'd learn about in business school or other professional education.

Just because these elements are somewhat expected doesn't mean they should be taken for granted. A leader who isn't intimately familiar with the enterprise's financial capabilities and limitations, its physical plant and equipment, or its position on the competitive playing field is a leader who is trying to play a game for which he or she lacks the basic equipment. I don't mean to suggest that the CEO of a Fortune 500 company necessarily needs to know how to repair the office heating and air conditioning equipment, but the CEO had certainly better know who is responsible for keeping the equipment running, how the expense of maintaining and using the equipment impacts the company, and what the recovery plan is should the equipment fail. Getting to know your enterprise's objective context may seem like dealing with the obvious—but it's still something that you absolutely have to do.

Context Is Subjective

There's a whole other dimension to the leadership context, and it's one that's often overlooked. It's what I think of as the "soft" assets of an enterprise: the way team members feel about their work; the intangible atmosphere shared by coworkers; the buy-in—or lack thereof—to the mission; the degree of shared ownership on the part of stakeholders. These, and many other subjective qualities, are every bit as much a part of the leadership context as the chart of accounts, the physical inventory, and the year-over-year change in market share. And a leader who would be truly great must make it his or her business to assess the subjective context every bit as carefully as the objective context.

Focusing on the subjective context can be especially challenging for leaders who are accustomed to taking the point, charging ahead, and relying mainly on their own intuitive sense of what ought to be done. For folks like these, it feels time-consuming, messy, and sometimes tedious to intentionally probe for the "soft" background.

We must always remember: We aren't leading assets—we are leading people. Human beings aren't chess pieces to be moved dispassionately here and there. Furthermore, leaders who attempt to manage human assets the same way they manage inventory control will usually find themselves frustrated, unsuccessful . . . or out of a job.

Why do you suppose the human context is almost endlessly variable and shifting? The answer is, because people change—from year to year, from day to day, sometimes even from moment to moment. Their priorities shift, based on their life circumstances. Their emotions cycle up and down, depending on what's going on in their personal, professional, and public lives. Their perceptions alter over time. For all these reasons, the human context is always moving, in a constant state of change.

Nevertheless, even though the human context is far more challenging to assess and understand than the more objective aspects of the leadership landscape, it is precisely the context to which leaders must attend most closely. The fact is that almost anything we accomplish as leaders is accomplished by, through, and for the people we lead. Organizations announce this principle so often that it has become a cliché, but that doesn't mean it isn't true: people are always your most important asset.

Think of any truly influential innovation, process, or movement: all of them involve people who got on board, made a commitment, and stayed the course until the vision became reality. As a leader seeking a breakthrough, your most important task is to accurately assess the subjective context in order to make sure those on your team are effectively contributing not only their time, but also their enthusiasm, their creativity, their imaginations, and their confidence.

> The fact is that almost anything we accomplish as leaders is accomplished by, through, and for the people we lead.

Acquiring this type of in-depth, constantly updated familiarity— especially where it concerns the subjective context—is difficult. Maybe that's one of the reasons why there is such a dearth of truly breakthrough leadership today. You must gently and repeatedly probe beneath the surface; you must not allow yourself to be satisfied with first appearances or easy answers. You must, in short, be a leader who is resolutely committed to assembling the strongest, most context-driven leadership framework possible for your organization. Only by making a commitment to relentless questioning of your own assumptions and perceptions will you avoid the contextual blind spots that can crop up in even the most mission-focused, energetic organizations.

The Gideon Model

Gideon was perhaps the most unlikely hero in the Bible. When God called him, as recorded in Judges 6, Gideon was hiding his wheat crop inside a wine press to keep it from being confiscated by the Midianites, a tribe of people who were oppressing Israel at the time. When God's messenger informed Gideon that he was to be the instrument of deliverance for God's people, his response was somewhat less than heroic: "How can I save Israel? My clan is the weakest in Manasseh, and I am the least in my family" (Judges 6:15). Not exactly a battle cry!

Once God finally convinced Gideon that he was the person for the job, Gideon was forced to focus very carefully on the human context of his leadership framework. When some 32,000 fighters answered his call to take up arms against the Midianite oppressors, God told Gideon, "You have too many men. I cannot deliver Midian into their hands, or Israel would boast against me, 'My own strength has saved me.' Now announce to the army, 'Anyone who trembles with fear may turn back and leave Mount Gilead'" (Judges 7:2–3). When Gideon, at God's direction, announced that anyone who was afraid could leave the army, 22,000 of them—two-thirds of his fighting force—took him up on it. Sort of makes you wonder why they mustered in the first place, doesn't it?

By now, Gideon had winnowed his enterprise down to the 10,000 fighters who said they weren't afraid. They were vastly outnumbered by the Midianites, but God still thought the human context wasn't right. He had Gideon take his army down to the water and instructed Gideon to eliminate all the men who got down on their knees to stick their faces in the water to drink, keeping only the ones who cupped water in their hands. By the time this rather strange training exercise was complete, Gideon was left with just 300 of the original 32,000 who answered his call. Talk about the few and the proud!

But there was one more piece to the human context that Gideon needed to know. Once again at God's prompting, Gideon infiltrated the vast Midianite camp at night. He overheard one of the Midianites telling another about a strange dream of destruction, and the listener said, "This can be nothing other than the sword of Gideon son of Joash, the Israelite. God has given the Midianites and the whole camp into his hands" (Judges 7:14). With this piece of vital military intelligence, Gideon went back to his army of 300 and made a plan. Later that night, they surrounded the Midianite camp and, on Gideon's signal, they blew trumpets and dashed pots to the ground, revealing flaming torches. The Midianite camp was thrown into utter confusion, and the tiny Israelite army routed the vastly superior forces of the oppressors.

None of this would have happened, of course, but for God guiding Gideon to a careful—if somewhat idiosyncratic—assessment of the context. General Gideon had precisely the right team assembled for the task at hand, and he also had an intimate understanding of the competitive environment. When the decisive moment came, he assembled the leadership framework in a way that created the breakthrough result he was seeking.

Now, it's highly unlikely that any of us will be so blessed as to receive a direct vision from God with directions for the success of our enterprise. But it is entirely likely that each of us will have the opportunity to carefully audit the context in which we are operating, examining it closely for the clues we need to assemble the right framework for leadership—the one that will lead to the breakthrough we seek.

CHAPTER THREE IN REVIEW

• Context drives and transforms meaning.

• Context is the raw material of the leadership framework.

• Context can be both objective and subjective.

• Accurately understanding the subjective context is often the more challenging task.

• The human context is constantly shifting; it requires frequent reassessment.

QUESTIONS FOR DISCUSSION

1. Think of a time when you had to adapt to a new context—at work, at school, in a social setting, etc. What changed? How did you feel?

2. What is the main challenge you face in learning to "read" people?

3. Can you think of ways you might assess a team member's emotional state? His or her enthusiasm or lack thereof? His or her level of commitment?

4. How important is it for leaders to continually assess their own emotional, intellectual, and mental context? How would that assessment affect their view of the total context?

CHAPTER FOUR

Clarity Is Contagious

*"I know you believe you understand what you think
I said, but I'm not sure you fully comprehend that
what you heard was not what I meant."*

—Anonymous

I t is said that one of the things that made Ulysses S. Grant a great general was the conciseness and clarity of his orders. In fact, most historians agree that one of the few non-debatable qualities of Grant, as general, president, and public person, was the extraordinary clarity of his written communications. Writers as diverse as Mark Twain and Gertrude Stein praised Grant's writing. In fact, in the closing weeks of his life, Grant labored through the agony of throat cancer to complete the manuscript for his two-volume *Personal Memoirs*, which became a posthumous bestseller—enough to permit his survivors to live in relative comfort, despite the fact that President Grant was in dire financial straits during his last years.[11]

Certainly, on the field of battle and enveloped by the "fog of war," there's no room for imprecise or unclear communication. When lives hang in the balance, it's imperative that leaders convey their orders, instructions, and guidance with the utmost conciseness and clarity.

But even in nonmilitary contexts, leaders must master the art of clear communication. In addition to setting forth the mission of the enterprise in unmistakable terms, effective leaders have the ability to communicate clearly the strategies and processes by which the mission is to be accomplished. They also connect with the people charged with carrying out those processes in a way that leaves no room for misunderstanding. They communicate expectations and responsibilities so that their hearers are in no doubt as to their part in the success of the organization. Finally, they have a crystal-clear understanding of how results will be measured and how vital feedback will be received, in order to accurately assess effort and make necessary adjustments. From the beginning of the communications process to the end of the final evaluation, effective leaders know how to maintain clarity throughout the enterprise. And perhaps even more important, they know how to cultivate that same clarity in the people around them.

Communications Complications

Of course, as we all know, clarity in communications is not as simple as saying what we mean. After all, the communication process doesn't involve only the communicator; it also involves the receiver of the communication. Just because what I say is completely clear and sensible to me, I cannot assume that you have accurately received the message I intended to send.

I have a friend who spent a number of years as a junior high school band director. He tells the story of his first day of teaching, after graduating from college. Though he had spent several weeks in the classroom prior to the beginning of school, trying to prepare the classroom environment and himself for what he would face when the students returned, he talks about that first day almost like someone who has survived a hurricane.

When the seventy or eighty junior high school students poured into the room, they immediately began pelting their new teacher with questions. Almost simultaneously, one student asked, "Do we need to get our instruments out today?" and another said, "Can I go to the gym for something?"

What the young teacher wanted to communicate was: (a) yes, the students needed to get their instruments out, and (b) no, the bell had rung and there was no time to leave the classroom to go to the gym. What he said out loud was, "No."

This simple, concise response had the beneficial effect of preventing the one student from kiting off to the gym without permission, but it also had the unfortunate effect of causing the other student to busily begin announcing to the others that no instruments would be needed that day.

The hapless young teacher communicated what he meant to say to the one student, but what the other students heard was the exact opposite of the teacher's intentions. Now, I will admit that a roomful of eager junior high kids on the first day back from summer vacation may not be the easiest place to cultivate clarity in communications, but the story makes the point that there is much more to the communication process than what is said; you must also consider what is heard.

Among other things, this fact points again to the importance of active listening, as we discussed in chapter two. One way to know for sure that what you intended to convey was actually the message received by the other person is by requesting feedback from the other person. There are many ways to do this: clarifying questions, reporting and reviews, and evaluations. Feedback can also be informal—even nonverbal, such as making good eye contact when speaking with someone, nodding or other body language that indicates acceptance or understanding, and short, verbal expressions that communicate recognition or agreement: "Yes . . . I've wondered the same thing . . . I hear you . . . I see why that's important . . . "

As a leader, you must be a careful, intentional observer, receiver, and provider of feedback. If you want to achieve maximum clarity in your communications, you need to learn to utilize feedback of all types in order to assess the accuracy of your communications.

For example, let's say you're concerned with the results being achieved in a certain department. You communicate your concern with the person responsible for that department, but by observing the nonverbal and verbal responses the individual offers to your communication, you conclude that the individual doesn't share your opinion of the seriousness of the problem. Based on this feedback, you would conclude that your communication hasn't been sufficiently clear. The message you intended to send hasn't been received. You need to find another, more effective way to make your point.

> As a leader, you must be a careful, intentional observer, receiver, and provider of feedback.

Great leaders, in addition to being practiced at active listening, are also typically good observers. When they communicate with team members, they are constantly watching for nonverbal clues as to how the message is being received. When team members speak, skilled leaders both listen and watch to gain perspective on not only what is being said out loud, but also the emotions, priorities, and intentions that propel what is being said. This is how they insure that members of the team are all supporting the mission—that they are all pulling in the same direction.

Clarity Unifies

In order to achieve breakthrough results, framework leadership utilizes clarity as a means of cultivating unified efforts from those in the organization. When a leader provides clarity of vision, clarity of mission, clarity of objectives, and clarity of process, that leader has created an environment that facilitates team members being on the same page. To put it another way, a climate of clarity, while providing good growing conditions for team unity, conversely

Clarity in the leadership framework permits a laser focus; it equips the organization to pursue success with relentless concentration.

discourages the growth of agendas that are not harmonious with the mission and vision of the leader.

I don't necessarily mean to imply that there are lots of people out there with unsavory intentions. The fact is that sometimes, people's goals, priorities, and intentions change. A person who was at one time completely on board with the mission and vision may, over time, become less enthusiastic or satisfied with continued participation. The more clarity afforded by the leadership, the more obvious it will be that this individual's interests no longer align with those of the enterprise as they once did. Good leaders will realize this and will take steps to help that individual find another situation that better utilizes his or her skills and talents and that better reflects his or her objectives, priorities, and passions.

Sometimes, too, it's necessary for leaders to differentiate between "good" and "best." An enterprise that is functioning with maximum clarity is constantly discerning between efforts that are absolutely central to achievement of its mission and those that, while perhaps worthwhile, are not at the core of what the organization is about. Clarity in the leadership framework permits a laser focus; it equips the organization to pursue success with relentless concentration.

Sir Christopher Wren and JFK

Tradition relates an incident involving Sir Christopher Wren, the architectural genius behind the building of St. Paul's Cathedral in London, and other monumental structures. It is said that a passerby asked a workman who was laboring on the site of the cathedral what he was doing, and the man replied, "I'm laying bricks." The same individual asked another workman what he was doing, and he replied, "I am helping Sir Christopher Wren build a cathedral to the Almighty."[12] Clearly, the second workman was the beneficiary of clarity surrounding the mission of which he was a part.

While it is unclear whether the anecdote of St. Paul's two workmen actually took place, the image and message of the story is powerful enough to travel through time, to 1962, where it germinated once again during the heady early days of the space race. It is reported that President Kennedy was touring a NASA facility, when he spotted a janitor doing some cleaning. He supposedly walked up to the janitor, asked the man what he was doing, and was told, "Mr. President, I'm helping to put a man on the moon."[13]

Though we may not be able to historically document either of these stories, we want to believe them, don't we? All of us yearn for the type of clarity and unity of mission that impels even those farthest down the organizational chart to engage their imagination and passion with the urgency of the shared vision. Like that bricklayer, we want to see our most humble efforts fitting into the big picture, helping to accomplish something great. Like the janitor, we want to believe that our small contribution to the organization is ultimately aiding the achievement of the grand objective.

But the only way to engage that type of buy-in at every level of the organization is to cultivate an environment of clarity. Leaders become great when this degree of clarity is a part of everything they say and everything they do. Clarity is the light that brings the vision into view; it's the glue that holds the leadership framework together.

CHAPTER FOUR IN REVIEW

• Clarity is essential to effective leadership communication.

• Great leaders cultivate clarity, not only in themselves, but also in those around them.

• Feedback is necessary to clarity in communications.

• Great leaders give, receive, and provide feedback.

• Clarity unifies; it helps everyone understand each individual's contribution to the success of the enterprise.

QUESTIONS FOR DISCUSSION

1. In your experience, what are some of the biggest obstacles to clarity in organizational communication?

2. How is feedback related to clarity?

3. Which do you think is more important: verbal feedback, or nonverbal feedback? Why?

CHAPTER FIVE

Alignment Accelerates

When we choose a goal and invest ourselves in it to the limits of concentration, whatever we do will be enjoyable.

—Mihaly Csikszentmihalyi

H ave you ever attended a concert by a fine orchestra? Quite possibly there's no better illustration of flawless organizational alignment than when a group of talented musicians works collectively to perform a masterwork by a great composer. And every now and then, something very special happens; a sort of mass magic takes over, and the performance is injected with a special quality that sets it apart even from other excellent renditions. The performers onstage can sense that a remarkable thing is happening—often, the audience can sense it as well. There's electricity in the air as performers and listeners are swept up together into an experience of timeless art being created in a manner beyond anything previously experienced: complete alignment, complete surrender to the spirit of the music and the ecstasy of the performance. It's the type of thing a professional musician may experience only a handful of times during an entire career, and it's unforgettable—a breakthrough to a whole new level.

Sometimes the same thing happens with sports teams. The players are in sync, almost as if they are reading each other's minds. Plays are executed flawlessly; people are in exactly the right places at the right times; the momentum seems unstoppable. When a team is perfectly aligned and hitting on all cylinders, it's amazing to behold—especially if it's your favorite team!

Psychologist Mihaly Csikszentmihalyi has studied the phenomenon that occurs when individuals or groups obtain the type of highly focused state described above. He calls it "flow."[14] As he describes it in the quote that opens this chapter, the experience of flow is perceived as pleasurable because when we are immersed in it, we are operating at a very high capacity, doing exactly what we intend to do. We don't experience the distraction or frustration that characterizes much of our day-to-day experience. We are, as the expression goes, "in the zone."

Like a sports team when everything is working right or an orchestra playing with skill and passion, an organization that is aligned will seem from the outside to be operating almost as a single unit—as if no real thought were involved. But of course, organizational alignment isn't at all a result of chance; it requires skillful communication, great clarity throughout the team, and purposeful, careful deployment of people, processes, and resources.

Alignment and Change

Alignment is never more important than when an organization is undergoing change. Let's face it: change, despite being the only constant, is usually a little scary. Change brings with it a heightened sense of urgency and awareness—sometimes, hyper-awareness. When the landscape is shifting, we are more apt to be on guard, watching for the fissures that might appear beneath our feet at any moment. When things around are changing rapidly—even chaotically—change becomes even more threatening. Mistakes become more likely. Problems become harder to solve.

However, when change is anticipated, the properly aligned organization can thrive, in spite of the shifting landscape. Leaders who carefully attend to alignment of people, strategies, processes, and resources create an engine for velocity amid change. They foster an environment where organizational flow can happen. In such enterprises, change—even rapid change—can actually energize, rather than intimidate. Framework leadership affords an organization not only clarity—the ability to perceive, all the way up and down the team, the correct priorities, actions, and attitudes—but also the alignment to execute the vision that has been defined. With proper alignment, execution can be adapted—"on the fly," if needed—to changing circumstances and assumptions. Clarity directs, defines, and prepares; alignment implements, responds, and maintains.

> **Leaders who carefully attend to alignment of people, strategies, processes, and resources create an engine for velocity amid change.**

Alignment Reflects the Leadership Framework

When an effective leader has invested the proper amount of time and effort in organizational alignment, the leadership vision is validated. A well-aligned team maintains momentum and, when necessary, recovers quickly from setbacks. It utilizes the clarity of shared vision in order to efficiently accomplish the steps leading to completion of the mission. When the leader has put in place the correct people, resources, and strategies, performance becomes a pleasure, both for the team and for other stakeholders. Like the orchestra and its audience, they are pulled into an unfolding experience of mutual benefit: one where things happen as they are supposed to happen and results provide the happy justification of prior preparation.

The principle benefit of good alignment, of course, is that it brings about a sense of flow: an environment where people are operating at high capacity without need for lots of managing or instructing. An aligned organization usually doesn't have to figure out how to respond—it just responds. Team members are free to do what they need to do in order to allow the organization to be what it needs to be. Strategies are in place that arise from clarity around the vision. Resources are allocated in harmony with the needs of the strategies. People perform in accordance with their strengths and their enthusiasms. And the organization and its stakeholders are the ultimate beneficiaries.

Alignment is one of the most important outcomes of the leadership framework; when the framework is correctly constructed and the enterprise is properly aligned within it, efficiency, effectiveness, and success are the results. As framework leadership encompasses the context and defines the mission and vision with clarity, it aligns all the components of the enterprise in a way that enables peak performance. With alignment, framework leadership paves the way for mission success. It eases the friction between current reality and accomplishment of the goal, and it increases positive momentum.

> **With alignment, framework leadership paves the way for mission success.**

David: An Aligned Leader

David is one of the most successful leaders portrayed in the Bible. I think that the secret to his success, especially in his early years, was his deep alignment with the purposes God had set out for him. David is a great example of a person who perceived his divine design and pursued it with passion. His leadership genius perhaps lay in the fact that he was able to inspire those around him to align with those same purposes.

David started his meteoric rise in pretty dramatic fashion: he killed a giant. And not just any giant; Goliath was huge, mean, well-armed, and a trained fighter. He was so intimidating that none of King Saul's seasoned warriors would attempt to face him. And yet David, though only a young boy at the time, went out to meet Goliath and was victorious because of his solid, simple faith in God and his alignment with God's call on his heart.

David quickly made a name for himself in the kingdom of Israel. As he added success to success, King Saul gave him greater and greater scope. And David always achieved results, because, as the Bible reports, "The LORD was with him" (1 Samuel 18:14). Saul had the wisdom to perceive David's alignment with God and to allow it full rein. David, in return, accomplished the mission that Saul had established.

But David's success came with a price. Eventually, David's fame and the admiration the common people held for him reached such high levels that Saul began to worry about his own personal security. Tragically, King Saul was unable to permit David to continue operating in the state of flow that resulted from his strong alignment with the will and intentions of God. Saul tried to kill David, who was forced to flee into the wilderness and live the life of a fugitive.

But even in exile, David proved his ability to inspire and lead. Soon, he gathered around him a team of experienced fighters and adventurers, and together they made for themselves a way of life. The core of the team became known as "David's

Mighty Warriors," and the core of the core, if you will, was a trio known as "The Three." Josheb-Basshebeth, Eleazar, and Shammah were their names, and they came to occupy a place in Hebrew lore somewhat akin to that of Davy Crockett, Daniel Boone, and Kit Carson. The twenty-third chapter of Second Samuel, in the Old Testament, tells of some of their exploits: feats of strength and courage in which they proved their loyalty to David and to his goals and objectives.

Ultimately, by remaining true to his alignment with God and his trust in God's purposes, David became the king of Israel, following Saul's death. David is described as a man after God's own heart (Acts 13:22), and because of his fundamental alignment with God's purposes, he became the most storied and beloved king of Israel.

Sadly, his life didn't end as well as it began. After a time, David's heart began to wander. He became more concerned with his own desires, trusted more in his own reputation than in remaining aligned with God's mission for his life. He even stole Bathsheba, the wife of Uriah, one of his most trusted lieutenants, and then had Uriah killed to cover up his sin. He failed to exercise proper leadership of his own children; one of his sons led an unsuccessful rebellion, and David experienced wrenching sorrow when his children even turned against each other in violence.

Alignment Requires Maintenance

One of the lessons in the story of David is that alignment isn't guaranteed to last forever. Just as your car requires periodic adjustment to make sure the wheels are properly aligned, so an organization's alignment must be carefully monitored and maintained. Also similar to an automobile, an organization's alignment can go astray by tiny increments. With your vehicle, things may seem to be going along pretty well, but over time, the tread on the tires starts to wear unevenly. If the alignment isn't corrected, you could be buying new tires a lot sooner than you need to. Similarly, your organization could be facing the need for a major overhaul that wouldn't have been necessary if you had made the small, incremental adjustments to alignment that would have kept things on track and running at peak efficiency.

As with clarity, maintaining alignment requires consistent, careful attention to feedback. One of the most important ways leaders can create a culture of useful feedback is by establishing a pattern of appropriate interaction among team members. This pattern must occur in a context of shared vision and mission, and it must involve various procedures that can be either formal or informal, as long as they encompass everyone necessary to the accomplishment of the mission—and as long as the pattern is consistent. When leaders establish such a pattern of meaningful interaction, and when they commit to careful, intentional focus on the feedback and monitoring of alignment characteristics up and down the team, they establish a pattern that provides a solid foundation for success.

CHAPTER FIVE IN REVIEW

• Alignment is both the result and the impetus for heightened and sustained effort, or "flow."

• Organizational alignment creates an atmosphere of achievement, satisfaction, and success.

• Alignment accelerates adaptation to change by freeing participants to respond in accordance with their potential and passion.

• Alignment is both essential to and an outcome of the leadership framework.

• Organizational alignment doesn't come with a lifetime guarantee; it requires periodic, purposeful maintenance.

QUESTIONS FOR DISCUSSION

1. Have you ever had to do a job or perform a function you felt unsuited for? How did it make you feel? What were your main difficulties?

2. How do you think leaders can best assess the proper alignment of people within the team? Alignment of resources? Alignment of strategies and procedures?

3. What are some signs of poor alignment among team members? As a leader, how would you address poor alignment?

CHAPTER SIX

The Power of Courage and Conviction

*There is nothing more difficult to take in hand, more perilous
to conduct, or more uncertain in its success, than to take
the lead in the introduction of a new order of things.*

—Niccolò Machiavelli, *The Prince* (1513)

J ames Earl Rudder was not a man you would expect to
espouse the cause of equality in educational opportunities
for woman and minorities. After all, he was a man's man who
grew up in the hardscrabble country of West Texas during
the 1920s and 1930s, who played football before facemasks
were invented. He loved coaching, and he loved leading
men, which he did with bravery and distinction during
World War II. Colonel James Earl Rudder's Second Ranger
Battalion was the outfit that scaled the treacherous cliffs
of Normandy's Pont du Hoc on D-Day, braving withering
enemy fire to disable the powerful gun battery mounted
there by the Wehrmacht.

Returning home to Texas as a war hero, Rudder began
rising through the ranks of leadership in his community and the

region, being elected Texas land commissioner in 1955. Then, in 1958, he was tapped to become president of his beloved alma mater, the Agricultural and Mechanical College of Texas—soon to become better known under Rudder's leadership as Texas A&M University.

Since its founding in 1871, Texas A&M had been a military training school limited to males. The college was justifiably proud of its record of having trained more officers for service in the two World Wars than any other institution except the U.S. Military Academy at West Point. The cadet tradition at Texas A&M was deeply entrenched and upheld with a nearly religious fervor by A&M alums—Aggies, as they call themselves—all over the nation.

But by 1958, the landscape of higher education was changing, and President Rudder knew it. More and more women were entering the workforce as professionals and were seeking a college degree. Rudder knew that in order to remain competitive, relevant, and compliant with developments in the courts, Texas A&M needed to become a coeducational institution. He also knew that the school's racial barriers would have to come down.

He further realized as well as anyone how the vast majority of Aggies would respond to any discussion of opening the school to enrollment by women and minorities or making military training non-mandatory. Most would label any such effort as the death knell of Texas A&M; the roar of outraged disapproval would be deafening.

It was a real problem. However, James Earl Rudder was not only visionary but courageous. After all, he had faced German artillery fire from the beaches of Normandy to the treacherous Colmar Pocket in western France. He wasn't one to back down from a challenge if he was convinced there was a job that needed to be done. And so, he set about quietly gathering support for a move to coeducation at Texas A&M. He cultivated state legislators and especially the governor, who appoints members to the university's Board of Regents. He began carefully building a coalition among friends and supporters of the school.

Despite all his careful planning and strategy, however, the divisiveness of the issue grew louder and louder, and as matters began coming to a head, Rudder received disparaging mail and faced harsh criticism in the public media. Old Aggies, some of whom had fought in World War I, threatened to send back their college rings, saying that Texas A&M was no longer the school they had graduated from. One former student even sent back his diploma, torn in two, with a note accusing Rudder of "selling out."

Through all the criticism, all the rancor, and all the bitterness, however, James Earl Rudder stayed the course. He pressed ahead, sought alliances, and maintained his insistence on doing what he firmly believed was best for the long-term future of Texas A&M. In 1963, Texas A&M admitted the first women students and the first African American students.[15]

Time has proven the wisdom of Rudder's courageous commitment. Today, more than 59,000 students study on the main campus, with thousands more enrolled at satellite campuses around the world. Texas A&M is a tier one research university offering more than 130 undergraduate programs, 170 master's programs, and 93 doctoral programs. And despite such dramatic growth, the university has retained its deep respect for tradition and for its beginnings.

James Earl Rudder knew that change was coming, and he knew that in order to survive and thrive, his organization would need to embrace and prepare for that change. At the same time, he knew that leading people through that change would require steadfastness, clarity, alignment, and the courage of his convictions. He was determined to position his organization for the shifting landscape, and he maintained that determination in the face of harrowing opposition. His courage and conviction were the sources of strength that enabled him to lead Texas A&M—sometimes with a lot of kicking and screaming—along the path to a breakthrough.

When It's Lonely at the Top

As the famous statesman Machiavelli noted in the opening quote of this chapter, leading change is both perilous and difficult. Yet, no breakthrough ever happens without going through change. Almost by definition, reaching the next level in any undertaking requires a process of change in order to move from "how it's always been" to where you really want to be. Framework leadership, then, requires the courage and conviction necessary to take the point during the process of change, even when the way forward looks uncertain and perhaps dangerous.

For this reason, framework leadership requires those qualities and processes that we have already discussed: (1) active, intentional listening; (2) careful, comprehensive attention to the context; (3) complete, consistent clarity around the mission and vision; and (4) studious attention to alignment in people, processes, and resources. When a leader has laid the all-important groundwork in these ways, and when that leader is thoroughly convinced that change is required or that a particular course of action is necessary, that thorough preparation becomes the basis for the leader's conviction. It gives the leader a reason to believe and to move forward with courage.

> Almost by definition, reaching the next level in any undertaking requires a process of change in order to move from "how it's always been" to where you really want to be.

Leading with Courage

But what if you've never led troops into battle or stormed an enemy stronghold like James Earl Rudder? What if you aren't sure you possess the type of courage needed to face the criticism and opposition that might come your way as you attempt to chart a course through change? Is courage only available to those who are born with it, or is it a skill, a state of mind, or a set of behaviors that can be learned?

Kathleen Reardon, in a 2007 article in the Harvard Business Review, asserts that courage is a skill leaders can adopt and also adapt to the needs of their circumstances. She says that courage may not necessarily involve a high-profile, do-or-die charge into the teeth of the enemy, as in the case of Rudder's action at Pont du Hoc. Instead, it may involve the sort of careful, behind-the-scenes consensus building he used to prepare for racial integration and co-education of women at Texas A&M. Certainly, leadership courage may involve drawing the proverbial line in the sand and staking everything on a single moment in time; it may also involve shrewd preparation

> Often, the crucial breakthrough depends on a leader having the courage and conviction needed to step forward in the face of uncertainty.

and choosing the right moment to make a move.[16] Astute leaders judge the situation they are facing and choose the proper means and moment to take their stand with the boldness needed to keep the organization on track for a breakthrough.

Often, the crucial breakthrough depends on a leader having the courage and conviction needed to step forward in the face of uncertainty. Especially in times when business conditions are difficult, when hunkering down seems like the prudent course, or when, for various other reasons, fear and avoidance of risk constitute the consensus wisdom, leaders with conviction and confidence can position their organizations to benefit most strongly when the environment improves. By communicating clearly and honestly even when they may not have all the answers; by stepping out in confidence, based on their belief in the preparation they've done, leaders with the courage of their convictions can put their organizations at the front of the line.

Significantly, business consultant and writer Susan Tardanico prominently lists good communications skills among the traits of courageous leaders, as profiled in her 2013 article for Forbes. Describing those who are able to maintain organizational momentum even in difficult times, Tardanico lists skills such as frequent and open communication (clarity); real-time, boots-on-the-ground understanding of the facts (contextual audit); and careful attention to feedback (active listening) among those she considers essential for leaders facing a difficult environment.

When You Can't See All the Way to the End

When I arrived at Southeastern University, I knew that some radical changes were needed. Enrollment was in decline, finances were shaky, and there was no sense of shared vision. There was no shortage of challenges.

Based on a careful analysis of what we heard from stakeholders, we came to the conclusion that several major initiatives would be pivotal in helping us get the university headed in a positive direction, such as starting a football program, designing a unique nursing program, and creating need-oriented education opportunities. We established new curricular and co-curricular programs to attract and retain motivated students who were serious about their goals.

Now, trust me when I tell you that neither of the above strategies—or, for that matter, any of the several other key initiatives we implemented as part of our vision for Southeastern—were inexpensive or risk-free. On one level, an outside observer might look at our startup football program or our campaign to establish and fund our nursing program and say, "Wouldn't it be better to take some baby steps first?" And such an opinion would have plenty of evidence to back it up—as a number of individuals pointed out to me in those early days.

But our leadership team was convinced that, even though there were many obstacles and uncertainties, these strategies were pivotal to placing Southeastern University on a path of steady growth, relevance, and leadership. So having done our homework and with much prayer (and a few deep breaths), we moved forward. Was the path perfectly clear? No. Did unexpected problems appear, and were there moments when success appeared unlikely? Certainly. But we "screwed our courage to the sticking place," as Shakespeare wrote. We persevered, and ultimately, our strategies began to accomplish what we had hoped they would.

The Secret Sauce

Leaders with the courage of their convictions are all too rare. Paradoxically, however, it is precisely in times that are most difficult and in environments that present the most obstacles that such leaders are most in demand. Organizations that can maintain their forward progress during the difficult times will always be at the forefront when conditions improve. And in order to do that, such organizations need leaders with courage and conviction to point the way, to motivate, to encourage, and to keep doing what is right, even when it is hard or seems like the wrong choice.

Remember that such courage isn't the same thing as

foolhardiness. No wise leader takes risks in situations where he or she doesn't fully understand the context, hasn't done the needed amount of listening, and hasn't paid proper attention to alignment. While it's true that it's impossible to know everything about everything, wise leaders will always do the necessary foundational work before moving forward.

Once the fundamentals are in place and the leader has done all that is reasonably possible to prepare, courage requires moving forward. Conviction enables that forward movement, even against obstacles and opposition. Leaders who can marshal these two qualities and model them for their organizations will inevitably rise to the top.

CHAPTER SIX IN REVIEW

• Leading in times of change is difficult.

• Courage and conviction propel leadership during uncertain times.

• Courage is a skill that can be practiced and adapted to the circumstances.

• Organizations that maintain momentum in hard times usually benefit most when conditions improve.

• Leadership courage is built on a foundation of thorough preparation.

QUESTIONS FOR DISCUSSION

1. What is the hardest decision you've ever had to make? What enabled you to make it? How did it work out? What, if anything, would you do differently now in the same situation?

2. What are the differences between courage and foolhardiness? How much information is enough, when a leader faces a difficult decision?

3. What is the relationship between preparation and conviction? What information do leaders need to make the right calls in hard times?

CHAPTER SEVEN

The Team Advantage

*Now this is the Law of the Jungle—as old and as true as the sky;
and the Wolf that shall keep it may prosper, but the Wolf that
shall break it must die. As the creeper that girdles the tree-
trunk, the Law runneth forward and back—for the strength of
the Pack is the Wolf; and the strength of the Wolf is the Pack.*

—Rudyard Kipling, 1895

As several wags have noted, there may not be an "I" in team, but there are an "M" and an "E." Anyone who has played organized sports, whether soccer in the local recreational league or high school or collegiate basketball, knows the "ball hog." This is the player who thinks the only way to score is to hang onto the ball and take the shot. Such individuals usually think of themselves—when they think at all—as the best player on the team and the only one who can do what needs to be done. They may even think they're leaders of a sort, but they aren't. No one who sees themselves individually as indispensable to the success of the team can ever be a truly effective leader. In fact, such types usually end up, eventually, as unsuccessful and frustrated, since no one wants to follow or listen to them.

If No One Is Following, You Aren't Leading

In most areas of worthwhile human endeavor, some sort of team is required. Even great, individualistic geniuses like Michaelangelo and Beethoven required the cooperation and efforts of others in order to become truly successful. Do you think that Michaelangelo quarried the stone for his iconic David all by himself? Did he transport it to Florence or build the scaffolding necessary to work on the gigantic piece of marble? Did Beethoven perform all the parts of his famous Fifth Symphony? Clearly, behind even monumental accomplishments that we most often associate with single persons, some sort of organization or team was needed.

> To the degree that you are able to assemble, coordinate, and inspire a team, you will be able to accomplish more of the great things to which you aspire.

This is certainly true today, whether we consider business and industry, education, scientific advancement, church work, or almost any other arena of human endeavor. Those who are most influential, who have the most impact, and who create the greatest breakthroughs, are most often those who have assembled an organization or team with the skills necessary to the effort at hand. To the degree that you are able to assemble, coordinate, and inspire a team, you will be able to accomplish more of the great things to which you aspire. On the other hand, if you lack the skills, temperament, or vision necessary to build and lead a team, your possibilities for impact are severely limited.

Team Building and Framework Leadership

The principles of framework leadership can function as a guide to building and maintaining the most efficient and appropriate team for your enterprise. Let's consider the elements in turn and see how they apply to putting together the organization that will create the breakthrough you seek.

First, drafting a winning team assumes that at some level, you have carefully considered the context in which your efforts are taking place. You have carefully reviewed the competitive environment, the opportunities available, the resources needed, and the challenges you are likely to face. You have looked within yourself and established the guiding principle or commitment that is both compelling and empowering you to accept the challenge before you. You know your own strengths and weaknesses, and you know the types of people needed to take both your strengths and your weaknesses into consideration.

As you consider the context and begin assembling the people needed to move forward, you listen carefully and actively. You realize that you can't effectively lead people whose views, motivations, and aspirations you don't understand. You listen and watch for the cues that can inform you as to what truly makes them tick and ignites their passions and most deeply held beliefs. As you interact with the team members, you consistently seek and focus on all types of feedback—verbal and nonverbal; formal and informal. In this way, you have maintained clarity around the mission and the strategies for accomplishing it. By staying in close communication with your team, you become more and more familiar with them, and they become more familiar with you. Familiarity leads to trust and to organizational agility.

Because you started with a good sense of the context and

because you paid careful attention to what your team members and prospective team members were telling you, you are able to achieve much greater alignment of your team with the vision and mission of the enterprise. People are in the right positions, with the right skills, interests, and passions, to move the enterprise forward. Resources, strategies, and procedures are well adapted to the effort. As much as possible, the team is poised to respond efficiently to difficulties and challenges.

Focus on alignment is especially important as you evaluate your team, your organization, and the steps and strategies needed to achieve breakthrough. Good alignment dictates that not only do you know where you are going, you also know what you will need to get there. Your team members, with their varying strengths, competencies, and interests, are your principal resource for achieving the goals of the enterprise.

Alignment and the Strength of Diversity

A musician friend of mine spent a summer playing in a Dixieland band. Now, Dixieland music may not be your particular cup of tea, but if you've ever heard a group of skilled Dixieland musicians, you've experienced a prime example of what happens when alignment happens among a group of people of diverse skills and abilities who are achieving a unified mission.

Sometimes, at first, an energetic Dixieland tune can sound like each musician is just doing his or her own thing—lots of notes, lots of energy, but so much going on at once that it's hard to pick out any particular tune. But when you listen closer, and especially if you're watching them play live, you start to see that everyone is listening to everyone else: The bass player and drummer are laying down a driving beat that each performer feels, bone-deep. The pianist is playing the chords that outline the musical territory of the tune. The horn players, though playing different melodic and rhythmic lines, are filling in the gaps for each other as their contributions combine to create something greater than the sum of the parts. Some musicians describe Dixieland as "unity in diversity," and that's pretty apt. Even though each player is creating independently of the others, to some degree, the group alignment around the tune, the beat, and the chord structure weaves it all together into a unified, aligned whole.

Notice that in the group there is a great diversity of approach and method. The trumpet player doesn't think the same way the drummer does, and the bass player and the trombonist are focused on different things. And yet, the contribution of each is essential to making the music sound the way it should.

It's the same way in any organization or enterprise. When a team is functioning as it should, individualism, rather than being lost or suppressed, is prized. The unique perspectives of each team member—results of differences in background, experiences, aptitudes, personal history, or what have you—contribute to the collective strength of the whole. One of the best things you can do for your organization, in fact, is to actively seek out people of varying backgrounds and interests.

Alignment is the key, of course. Just throwing a bunch of diverse people into a room is no guarantee that anything great is going to happen, any more than tossing a bunch of tiny gears and moving parts into a bucket will make a clock. But when those people are aligned with a mission that has been articulated with clarity, something great is guaranteed to happen! When they're inspired, energized, and empowered by a skilled leader, breakthroughs are in the making.

When a team is functioning as it should, individualism, rather than being lost or suppressed, is prized.

When the Game Changes, the Team Responds

Dealing with change—even individual change—almost always requires some sort of team response. When we go through challenging changes in life, for example, we usually turn to someone for help: a pastor, a counselor, or even a trusted friend. And organizational change is no different. The best teams deal with change in a smooth, coordinated way, responding organically, up and down the organization. Aligned individuals, working within aligned groups, are able to take their cue from the leadership and respond to change, in accordance with the overall mission. Notice that a single enlightened, passionate leader isn't enough; a team response is required to incorporate the changing situation into an evolving, vision-centered response.

I like the image of a unified, yet diverse team that the apostle Paul presents in his first letter to the Christians at Corinth. Paul was addressing a team—the Corinthian church—that was acting like anything but a team! These folks were wrangling over all sorts of things, and one of Paul's main purposes in writing his letter to them was to remind them of how they were supposed to be aligned, with each other and, most importantly, with Jesus, the great Leader whom they were to follow.

It seems, though, that the Christians at Corinth were more interested in establishing a pecking order of value than in carrying out the mission. The world was changing around them, but they were too busy trying to show each other how great and indispensable they were to get about the business of aligning with the mission.

In 1 Corinthians 12:12 and the following verses, Paul tells the Corinthians that the church—the "team," if you will—is like the human body. Our bodies have many different parts that carry out vastly different functions: the eyes don't look anything like the heart, and the nose doesn't even faintly resemble the hands. And yet, each part has its proper place in the body and is essential for the smooth functioning of the whole. As Paul puts it, "If the whole body were an eye, where would the sense of hearing be? If the whole body were an ear, where would the sense of smell be? . . . The eye cannot say to the hand, 'I don't need you!' And the head cannot say to the feet, 'I don't need you!'" (1 Corinthians 12:17, 21).

We can see Paul's point clearly. The body can't function if the parts don't work together in harmony, each in its unique way. And yet, too often, teams—especially when confronted by the stress of change or new challenges—start to break down because the members fail to appreciate the strength that lies in diversity.

However, when team members are aligned under the guidance of a skilled and visionary leader who communicates with clarity, listens with focus and intention, and pays close attention to the evolving context, change can become the catalyst for truly amazing transformation. Such teams become alliances of change agents, embracing developments as they occur and incorporating them into the ever-transforming strategy for realizing the organizational vision. When the game changes, the great teams change with it. By adapting to and embracing change, they make change an integral part of their success.

CHAPTER SEVEN IN REVIEW

• Leaders can't go it alone; they need the help of a great team in order to execute the mission.

• Framework leadership incorporates the skills needed to assemble a high-functioning team.

• The best teams incorporate and appreciate diversity.

• Aligned, unified teams accept change as a catalyst rather than a threat.

QUESTIONS FOR DISCUSSION

1. The last time there was a major change at your office or workplace, how did you respond? Why do you think you responded this way?

2. Can you think of someone in your organization who is the image of a "team player"? What qualities go into making this person fit this description?

3. What do you think is most valuable in a team member: talent or alignment?

4. How might your attitude toward change be affected by your attitude toward your team?

CHAPTER EIGHT

Balancing Urgency with Vision

Make haste slowly.

—Desiderius Erasmus, 1466–1536

In 1954, President Dwight D. Eisenhower addressed the Second Assembly of the World Council of Churches, meeting in Evanston, Illinois. Somewhere around the halfway point of his speech, while discussing the problems currently faced by humanity and the importance of the churches in helping to solve those problems, Eisenhower made this statement: "I have two kinds of problems, the urgent and the important. The urgent are not important, and the important are never urgent."

President Eisenhower attributed the adage to another president, J. Roscoe Miller, then president of Northwestern University, located right there in Evanston. Eisenhower went on to express his hope that the world religious leaders gathered before him could, by drawing upon the power and perspective of faith, help to focus the leaders of the world on what was really important and even, in his words, to "give the important the touch of urgency."[17]

Bestselling author and consultant Stephen Covey, with Roger Merrill and Rebecca Merrill, later refined this statement by President Eisenhower into what he called the "Eisenhower Decision Matrix." In their book *First Things First*, Covey, Merrill, and Merrill specified four quadrants: (1) important and urgent; (2) important but not urgent; (3) not important, but urgent; and (4) not important, not urgent. They proposed this matrix as a way of prioritizing tasks and decisions that leaders and others must make.[18]

Sure, "Haste Makes Waste," But . . .

Clearly, President Eisenhower and, later, Covey and his coauthors, were onto an important principle. And at least as far back as the second century BC, people have known that sometimes, when you get in too big a hurry, you end up making more work for yourself. The Jewish Book of the Wisdom of Sirach says, "There is one that toileth and laboureth, and maketh haste, and is so much the more behind" (11:11). More modern proverbs making the same point are numerous: "Slow and steady wins the race" . . . "The hurrier I go, the behinder I get" . . . "If you don't have time to do it right, when will you have time to do it over?"

It's your responsibility as a leader to pull the team's focus back to the important rather than allow their attention to be claimed by the shrill demands of the urgent.

But it's difficult to remember these sayings in the heat of battle, isn't it? When we are faced with the urgent—the report that has to be on the boss's desk first thing in the morning; the presentation for the board of directors in two days; the auditors who showed up this morning, asking for everyone's travel records—all too often, the important goes out the window. We become reactive instead of proactive. We start seeing the alligators circling around us in the water, and our original objective of draining the swamp is lost in an urgent desire for safety.

However, framework leadership requires that you maintain your focus on the important—those priorities, strategies, and efforts essential to attain the vision—and not be continually distracted by what author Charles Hummel calls the "tyranny of the urgent." Oh, certainly, there are times in any organization when you must do damage control. As the leader, you will be called on for a response to the unforeseen emergencies that happen in the life of every enterprise.

But you must always return to your focus on the ultimate mission. You must not allow the urgent to consistently dictate the agenda. It's your responsibility as a leader to pull the team's focus back to the important rather than allow their attention to be claimed by the shrill demands of the urgent.

Change and Urgency

But what about those times when change is taking place and responding to the altered landscape is the difference between mission success and failure—or between survival and demise? In such cases, shouldn't leaders get behind the wagon and push a little, if necessary, to move things along?

Not always. Especially with legacy organizations, where the leader is attempting to move the enterprise in a different direction or at a different pace than what it has been accustomed to, too much pushing and shoving can, once again, become counterproductive to the ultimate goal.

This is where the skilled leader deploys to the fullest the skills of listening, clarity, and seeking feedback. He or she pays close attention to the human context, noticing not only where resistance to change is occurring, but doing the utmost to understand the backgrounds of that resistance in each individual case. Remember our earlier discussion of leadership courage, when we noted that while there is a time for leading a dramatic charge against the barricades, there is also a time for careful strategy and building of consensus. Sometimes, when leaders attempt to push and prod team members along in a direction they're unfamiliar with or don't have the capacity for, both leaders and team members do more harm than good.

It's also true that sometimes the pace of change isn't readily apparent from the outside, looking in. Even when you've listened to your team members and solicited their feedback, you can't be 100 percent certain about the processes taking place within them as they encounter and negotiate change. What may seem a simple, logical matter to you, might be, for reasons you don't understand, a huge mental or emotional obstacle to a team member. That this individual is staying engaged at all may be a huge victory in the team member's eyes, even though to you it may seem that he or she is moving at a glacial pace.

For example, let's suppose that one of your strategies for managing change is a new cloud-based software package that will enable you to manage stakeholder relationships more quickly and efficiently. You've done the research, you've compared products, and you've talked to users of the system; you're convinced that switching over to this system will help the organization address some of the current problems.

But what you don't realize is that in a previous work situation, one of your team members was downsized out of a job, with the reason given as redundancy created by greater technological efficiency. In other words, the reason you are changing software systems is the same reason that cost your team member a previous job.

Can you understand why this particular team member might not be as enthusiastic about the technology upgrade as everyone else? Now, it may be that you know that this particular team member will be crucial to the way you plan to implement the new system. But until that person knows this and understands how the change will affect them personally, you'll have a hard time getting their buy-in.

Does this rather simplistic example help you understand why listening, clarity, and feedback are so important when guiding an organization through a change process? The issues at stake can be much more complex than the hypothetical situation above, and that just means that as the leader, your responsibility is greater and more nuanced.

Another factor is that the phase of the change process affects how change is perceived. Typically, at the beginning of a process of change, things will seem to be moving very slowly, if at all. However, in the latter stages the process can seem to be moving rather quickly. It's all about inertia and momentum, as Isaac Newton told us long ago. Inertia is difficult to overcome, but once it is overcome, momentum takes over and the process moves at a brisk pace. Leaders need to remember this principle and exercise care about the pace at which they insist upon implementing change within the enterprise.

A Word of Caution

While my clear intention with this chapter is to counsel leaders to allow the long-term strategy—rather than short-term emergencies—to set the pace of the agenda, there are clearly times when urgency determines the momentum. In other words, there will certainly be times in most organizations when leaders have no choice but to attend to the urgent, or there will be no opportunity to execute the long-term strategy. Just as an emergency room doctor must stop the patient's arterial bleeding before worrying about his high blood pressure, there are times when leaders must take action to save the enterprise, even if they haven't gained full clarity and alignment.

When I came to Southeastern University, for example, the school faced several issues that would have meant the death of the enterprise if they had continued unaddressed. We had diminishing enrollment; we had inadequate systems in place that needed immediate overhaul; we had a culture of estrangement creating alienation among some vital constituencies; and we were bleeding red ink. Any one of these problems can bankrupt a university—and has. Before our leadership team could put in place any long-term, strategic initiatives, we had to take steps to make sure the university would be in existence for the long term!

> There will certainly be times in most organizations when leaders have no choice but to attend to the urgent, or there will be no opportunity to execute the long-term strategy.

Once those urgent problems were addressed, we were able to turn our focus to developing the people, systems, and organization necessary to our leadership framework. In other words, once we attended to the urgent, we could turn to the more deliberate, proactive pace that characterizes leadership meant to last for the long haul.

Time Is Not the Enemy

When I think of great leaders and the importance of not rushing things, I recall what Jesus told His followers in Mark 6. The background is that He had just sent His disciples out on a mission to teach and heal. They were fulfilling the mission their leader had envisioned for them, and it was a very exciting time. The gospel of Mark tells us, "They went out and preached that people should repent. They drove out many demons and anointed many sick people with oil and healed them" (Mark 6:12–13). It was a thrilling period in the lives of these disciples as the kingdom of God was being launched.

Naturally, when they returned to where Jesus was, they were eager to report on what had happened. After all, there was profound change afoot; things were moving quickly in the direction that Jesus had outlined for them.

But it was too much. The pace was too hectic, and Jesus knew it. Mark's gospel reports, "because so many people were coming and going that they did not even have a chance to eat, he said to them, 'Come with me by yourselves to a quiet place and get some rest'" (Mark 6:31). Jesus knew His followers needed some time to catch their breath, to think quietly about all the changes they had witnessed. So He took them by boat to a solitary place.

The trouble was, people spotted them leaving, and by the time they got to their "retreat center" the place was already mobbed by a crowd of eager miracle-seekers. What follows is the famous story of Jesus feeding the five thousand with five loaves and two fish.

The point for our purposes is this: Jesus, as the disciples' leader, knew when things needed to slow down a bit. He could tell that His followers—His "team"—needed some space, a respite from the rapid pace of change.

Some leaders aren't so wise. Some believe that it's best to "keep up the momentum" and even push harder. And sometimes, that can be the right decision. But other times, leaders need to take a page from Jesus' playbook. Sometimes, the leader needs to allow things to slow down, to recognize that time spent in quiet and contemplation is not time wasted. Sometimes, successfully leading a team through a process of change means you allow the pace to slow down so they can assess and accept the evolving context. Such a leader recognizes that time, rather than being an enemy, can be an organization's best ally.

CHAPTER EIGHT IN REVIEW

• Leaders should never confuse the urgent (short-term, tactical considerations) with the important (long-term, strategic, mission-centered considerations).

• It can be difficult to keep the long-term, strategic perspective when dealing with the urgent, but leaders must retain their focus on the important.

• Leaders must carefully assess how much change to attempt at one time, with special consideration for the human context. Active listening, clarity, and feedback are key to this assessment.

• Effective leaders balance the pace of change with the organization's ability to effectively understand and incorporate the change being made.

QUESTIONS FOR DISCUSSION

1. Think of an occasion when you became impatient with someone's response or actions, only to learn later that the person had a valid reason for acting as they did. How do you wish you had handled that situation differently? What could you have done, if anything, to better understand the full situation?

2. Have you ever felt the need to "step away" for a while at work when things were hectic? What caused you to feel that way? What did you do that enabled you to remain effective and engaged?

3. Think of a time when you believed changes were being made that were not warranted. Did your opinion alter as you went through the process? If it did, what caused you to change your mind?

CHAPTER NINE

Facing Failure

"I've missed over 9,000 shots in my career. I've lost almost 300 games. Twenty-six times I've been trusted to take the game-winning shot and missed. I've failed over and over and over again in my life. And that is why I succeed."

—Michael Jordan

Let me list a few names for you, and see how many of them you recognize: Oprah Winfrey, Walt Disney, Thomas Edison, Abraham Lincoln, J. K. Rowling, Bill Gates, Stephen Spielberg, Tom Landry, Charlie Chaplin, and, last but not least, Michael Jordan. All of these folks share some common traits: each of them rose to the top ranks of an incredibly competitive field of endeavor; each of them and their work is known to millions upon millions of people all around the world . . . and each of them failed miserably, multiple times.

What do you imagine was going through Bill Gates' mind, for example, as he contemplated the flop of his first business, Traf-O-Data? The concept was to use computers (as they existed in 1972) to read the raw data from pneumatic traffic counters and repackage the data for local and state traffic engineers. The only problem was that when Gates and his partners finally got a chance to demonstrate their prototype to a potential customer—it didn't work. Gates next decided to go to college and entered Harvard in 1973, only to drop out two years later. Why did he drop out? To start a little company called Microsoft.

We already know what Michael Jordan thinks, based on his opening quote.[19] This superstar learned the principle that led to a career that included multiple MVP awards, six NBA championships, and a designation by ESPN as the greatest North American athlete of the twentieth century. The principle is this: the secret of success is failure.

Failure and the Change Process

Allow me to assure you of one unalterable fact: the only way to avoid failure is to attempt nothing. It's like the old story of the farmer, standing around at the local feed store. Everybody else was busily going in and out, getting needed supplies so they could get back to work on their farms. But this fellow was standing and watching, apparently with nothing much that needed doing.

One of the other farmers finally asked him, "Aren't you going to go plant cotton?"

"Nope," he replied. "I don't plan to make a cotton crop this year; I'm afraid of the boll weevils."

"Well, then I guess you're getting ready to harvest your wheat."

"Didn't plant wheat, either. Worried about the army worms."

"Then I suppose you're waiting until it's time to plant corn."

"Not planting corn; think there might be a drought."

"Well," the exasperated friend finally said, "it sounds like you're not doing any farming this year."

"That's right; I decided to play it safe."

We can all see the obvious flaw in this reasoning. If you never try, you can't fail—except that failure to try is the greatest failure of all.

This is especially true when an enterprise is going through a process of change. Failure is not only inevitable within the change process; it's integrally connected to its success. Negotiating change, especially in an organization, is a complex process, fraught with unknowns and uncertainties. No matter how well aligned the team, how good the communication, how pervasive the clarity, and how thoroughly the context is understood, there will be failures: blind alleys, ideas that don't pan out, inappropriate strategies, products that don't work as anticipated . . . you name it, and there's a way it can go wrong.

Should that scare you, as a leader? Well, maybe a little. Remember, there's a difference between courage and foolhardiness. But the likelihood of failure should never deter you from the persistent pursuit of the vision. In fact, those individuals—like the people listed at the beginning of this chapter—who can experience failure, learn from it, and use those lessons as the next stepping-stone—are those who usually make the greatest breakthroughs. They are the ones we admire most, not because they never failed, but because they wove their failures into ultimate success.

Failure and the Leader's Heart

By their very nature, of course, most leaders take failure personally. They see it as an indictment of their wisdom, their abilities, their planning, or their ability to communicate. They feel failure keenly; it strikes at the heart of their confidence in themselves and their vision.

But when failure happens—and it will—the skilled and resilient leader recognizes it as an opportunity for learning and improvement. As Edison concluded in his quest for a working electric bulb, when one method has conclusively proven unsuccessful, it can be eliminated and the search for the successful method can continue. Leaders must train themselves to see a failure in the context of the overall effort. Very often, failures contain the seeds of ultimate success.

The last thing a leader should do, in fact, is try to ignore, hide, or gloss over failure when going through a change process. This may be tempting sometimes, especially when the change being implemented is one that was viewed negatively by one or more team members. In such situations, the leader's natural tendency may be to try to hide or minimize the failure to avoid providing ammunition for those who might like to shoot holes in the change process.

> When failure happens—and it will—the skilled and resilient leader recognizes it as an opportunity for learning and improvement.

But by acknowledging the failure, dissecting it, taking the available lessons to heart, and creating a new plan based on the available information, leaders can often earn the respect of those who might otherwise be inclined to be naysayers. When team members see that leadership holds itself accountable and deals openly with failure, buy-in can actually increase.

The point is that leaders should not harness their personal value to some idea of an unbroken string of successes. They should also not equate their value to the organization or the validity of their vision with their ability to avoid failure. Such expectations on the part of leaders—or followers—are unrealistic, unattainable, and ultimately defeating

A Temporary Detour Isn't the End of the Road

The principle behind the change process is one that is well known to therapists and counselors: If you keep doing what you've always done, you'll keep getting what you've always gotten. So, the imperative for accepting the challenge of change is pretty hard to ignore. If your enterprise is going to experience the breakthrough success you've envisioned, it can't keep doing things the way it always has.

This means that as a leader, you must prepare yourself and your team for the fact that failure is integral to the change process. As your organization moves from "how-it's-always-been" to the breakthrough you've envisioned, there will be problems—some anticipated, and some that are impossible to anticipate.

> As a leader, you must prepare yourself and your team for the fact that failure is integral to the change process.

At this point, it might be useful to recall the Eisenhower Principle: Does this failure represent the urgent, or the important? If it's a problem around a short-term objective or process, it's probably urgent, but not important, and you should prioritize it accordingly. But if the failure represents a flaw or miscalculation in a fundamental, strategic component, it's important, and you should manage it with all the seriousness it deserves.

The idea is to not allow a temporary setback to distract you from the long-term vision. You must not allow the urgent to dictate your decisions, to the detriment of handling the important. Fortunately, leaders with well-aligned teams who have created great clarity around the mission and vision can usually negotiate mishaps, when they occur, with efficiency and minimal upset to long-term strategy. The key is to build a team characterized by mutual respect and confidence, from top to bottom. When a team has these qualities, it can accept the uncertainty that inevitably accompanies innovation. Team members have less anxiety and more willingness to try different methods and procedures when they know they can rely on each other and on their leaders. If something doesn't work, they have confidence they can absorb the failure, learn from it, and move on.

"Failure is a necessary part of the innovation process," writes Edward D. Hess of the Darden Graduate School of Business at the University of Virginia, "because from failure comes learning, iteration, adaptation, and the building of new conceptual and physical models. . . . Almost all innovations are the result of prior learning from failures."[20] As a leader negotiating the change process that paves the way to a breakthrough for your organization, you will certainly face failure. But with the right attitude and preparation, failure can become, as Michael Jordan says, a building block of ultimate success.

CHAPTER NINE IN REVIEW

• Some of the world's most successful and influential people have failed, spectacularly and often.

• The learning that comes through failure is indispensable to improvement.

• Failure is an integral part of the change process.

• Failure isn't necessarily an indictment of the leader's vision, abilities, or skills.

• Leaders must not allow short-term difficulties to distract them from the long-term strategy.

QUESTIONS FOR DISCUSSION

1. In your life, what failure has affected you most deeply? What did you learn from it?

2. In your opinion, what separates those who learn from failure and ultimately succeed from those who are derailed or destroyed by it?

3. How can a leader judge if a failure is urgent or important in its effect on the organization? How should the leader's response differ in the two categories?

CHAPTER TEN

Beyond the Edge of Possibility

*For, you see, so many out-of-the-way things had
happened lately, that Alice had begun to think that
very few things indeed were really impossible.*

—Lewis Carroll, *Alice's Adventures in Wonderland*

How do you make a map for a place you've never been? This question confronts every leader who seeks to position an organization for a breakthrough. Because, when you think about it, any change process that leads to a breakthrough is fundamentally about going on a journey from the known to the unknown. No great leader ever said, "My goal for this enterprise is to be doing the same things the same way in five years."

Honestly, it isn't an option to stay where you are, if for no other reason than that the earth is spinning—and carrying you with it—at a speed of between 700 and 850 miles per hour, depending on how far north of the equator you happen to be. Clearly, to achieve anything great, change is both the doorway and the path. As a leader, it's up to you to inspire and enable your team to walk through that door and down that path, into the unknown—where the breakthrough awaits.

Yet, we all know that change of any kind—and especially organizational change—brings with it not just possibility, but also a certain amount of fear. How do leaders balance these two opposite pulls as they lead a team through a process of change?

Sailing Off the Edge?

We all learned in elementary school that Christopher Columbus "sailed the ocean blue" and landed in the New World in 1492. Many of us were also taught that Columbus's voyage "proved" the world was actually not flat, despite the supposed near-mutiny of crew members who thought they were sailing to their deaths. In all probability, Columbus, like the other educated people of his day, was familiar with philosophers' and geographers' theories of a round earth that date back to at least the sixth century BC.

But what Columbus clearly didn't know was the size of the ocean he was attempting to cross. In fact, he was searching for an alternate route to India and the Malay Archipelago that didn't involve making the dangerous passage around the Cape of Good Hope. He didn't realize that he had an entire hemisphere between him and his intended destination.

So, in a manner of speaking, you could call Columbus a colossal failure. After all, he didn't accomplish his original goal. However, he did accomplish something pretty amazing— something that would never have happened without the exercise of vision, determination, leadership, and resilience.

I think Columbus also had another important factor in his favor: He had a leadership framework. He had clarity around his goals; he was familiar with the context, as far as current knowledge permitted; he strategically positioned his resources; he achieved sufficient alignment to maintain the needed level of cooperative effort; and he demonstrated enough courage and conviction to motivate the efforts of the team he had assembled, even though the way was unknown. Despite not achieving his original intention, he still accomplished something that changed the world.

Framework leadership gives the leader a kind of map of the unknown. It provides a structure, a rationale, and a method for moving an organization forward in the change process, even when the destination may be unclear. It functions as a tool for managing both the possibilities that change offers and the fear of the unknown that change summons. And it provides a bulwark for the leader's

Framework leadership gives the leader a kind of map of the unknown.

commitment to the vision and the courage to pursue it. Just as Columbus used the navigational tools available to him to chart—or keep track, at least—of his progress across the ocean, so framework leadership permits a leader to continue pursuing the vision, even if the route is unfamiliar.

It also gives the leader a way to respond to the unexpected. Columbus eventually realized that the beach he was standing on was not anywhere in Asia. However, he was able to make the necessary shift to realize that, though the result of the voyage was unexpected, there were still benefits to be gained.

In fact, many of the products we depend on today are the results of accidents similar to the one that landed Columbus in the Caribbean instead of the Moluccas. Vulcanized rubber (without which car tires would either melt in the heat or freeze stiff in the cold), penicillin (the godfather of all modern antibiotics), microwave ovens (the mainstay of breakrooms everywhere), Velcro (delaying for years the need to tie your shoes), and Teflon (the salvation of many an omelet) are just a few of the things we take for granted that were discovered by people who were actually looking for something else.

We might conclude that the journey through the change process may yield benefits that no one—including the leader—has yet imagined. But these benefits will never materialize without framework leadership—the principal tool that visionary leaders need to negotiate the path through the unknown.

The fundamental aspects of framework leadership—listening, contextual understanding, clarity, and alignment—are a leader's most dependable assets when moving an organization through a process of change. They enable the type of relationships, up and down the team, that make for nimble responses to unexpected developments. They also lead to trust and interdependence in the organization, which usually results in high morale, even in the face of uncertainty. When you know you can depend on the people around you, and you know that they share the same motivation and vision that you do, you are more willing to step forward, even if you can't be entirely certain what the footing is like.

If You Aren't Moving Forward, You're Getting Behind

You've probably heard the commonly repeated belief that sharks must swim constantly in order to obtain oxygen from the water, since they lack the mechanism to pump water over their gills. Marine biologists inform us that this isn't entirely true, but the image is appropriate for understanding the nature of innovation; innovators must constantly innovate, or they cease to be relevant.

We believe this implicitly at Southeastern University. Each year, our leadership team goes on a retreat with the sole purpose of defining the next two or three things that we must do to achieve the next breakthrough. We believe we can't afford to rest on our past successes; we must constantly achieve the next innovation. Only in this way can we maintain breakthrough momentum.

One of the problems I see in many legacy organizations is that they've become comfortable. Usually, they've enjoyed some level of success, and the leadership mindset has become one of maintaining that comfort level, rather than venturing out into the unknown in search of the next breakthrough. Time and again, business history demonstrates that when industry-leading organizations become complacent in their position, they lose that position. I believe there is simply no option other than continuous innovation, a persistent quest for the next potential breakthrough—that is, if the enterprise intends to continue thriving for the long term.

In 2013, Nokia sold its mobile phone division to Microsoft. What makes this remarkable is that at one time, Nokia was perhaps the world's most dominant manufacturer of mobile phones; some calculate that more than 50 percent of the world's mobile phones were Nokia. And yet, by 2013, they had lost such overwhelming market share to the iPhone and other smart phones that the mobile phone business was no longer tenable for them.

At the end of the press conference announcing the sale, the CEO of Nokia made a statement I find chilling: "We didn't do anything wrong, but somehow, we lost."[21] In other words, by failing to continue to innovate and seek the next breakthrough, Nokia's mobile phone division settled for maintaining a successful status quo. As a result, they became irrelevant—and they failed.

Innovation, Risk, and Framework Leadership

Leaders seeking breakthroughs in their enterprises, whether operating in a business, not-for-profit, religious, educational, or even governmental context, must always be conscious of the tradeoffs between innovation and risk. When you are attempting to do what has not been done before, or to do what has been done but in a way it has never been done, you are, by definition, an innovator. And all innovators must become comfortable with the uncertainties that go along with venturing into unfamiliar territory. By applying the principles of framework leadership, you'll have a means of judging the variables of a contemplated change process. You'll be able to assess the context and decide if the potential reward justifies the uncertainties you must accept to gain it.

Once the risk has been assessed and judged appropriate to the potential reward, innovative leaders must assemble diverse teams. They know that to come up with the type of dynamic innovations they seek, they need people of widely varying temperaments, viewpoints, skill sets, and backgrounds. Sometimes this means that a team member may have viewpoints that don't match yours very well. But if alignment with the mission is there, that "outside" viewpoint may perceive the critical next step toward breakthrough. After all, alignment doesn't mean conformity; it means collective effort in a common direction.

> **Innovative leaders must be able to trust their team members.**

Innovative leaders must be able to trust their team members. This is one of the principle functions of maintaining a focus on alignment. They must trust the members of their team, even when they don't always agree with them. And they must permit team members the leeway, within the broad context of organizational alignment, to pursue efforts that may not immediately make sense to the leader. If there is clarity around the vision, and if alignment is in place, this atmosphere of "creative chaos" can result in the type of discoveries and innovations that bring about breakthroughs. Conversely, if everyone on the team is looking at the same things in the same way, the team loses the opportunity for the fresh insights that lead to successful innovation.

Innovative leaders are unceasingly curious. They probe; they ask questions; they test assumptions. They also encourage team members to be the same way. Innovation is often a process of asking "what if" questions of parts of the process that most assumed were settled long ago.

Innovative leaders know when to get out of the way. This quality goes along with team alignment and diversity. Skilled leaders recognize that, sometimes, the best leadership style involves the confidence to allow a team member to follow a lead to its conclusion.

Innovative leaders always draw the focus back to implementation. After all, the greatest concepts in the world can't change anything until they're implemented in some practical, real-world way. Framework leadership demands that the results not only justify the effort, but also meaningfully advance the mission.

Finally, innovative leaders are always listening, always soliciting and absorbing feedback. This is the constant input to the leadership framework that great leaders place above all else. Leaders who never assume they have all the answers or all the information, who are consistently attentive to the environment, the people, and the data, are the ones best positioned for the critical insights that lead to breakthroughs. They know that when sailing in uncharted waters, the only security is awareness. They not only practice awareness themselves, but also enable and promote it in others.

CHAPTER TEN IN REVIEW

• Positioning an organization for a breakthrough necessitates leading it through unknown territory.

• Change brings with it not only possibility, but also fear.

• Leaders must balance uncertainty and opportunity as they lead the change process.

• Great breakthroughs necessitate a certain amount of risk.

• Framework leadership enables innovation while managing risk.

QUESTIONS FOR DISCUSSION

1. How does a leader's confidence impact a team undergoing a change process?

2. Which quality do you think is more important for innovation: vision or operational acumen? Why do you think so?

3. In your opinion, how should a leader assess risk versus reward?

Positioned for a Breakthrough

Great joy in camp; we are in view of the ocean, this great Pacific Ocean which we have been so long anxious to see.

—Journal of Lt. William Clark, November 7, 1805

As we come to the end of our journey through framework leadership, it's important to recall our point of origin: God has a divine design for your life. You carry within you the imprint of God; you are made in His image. Just as God is creative, you are creative. Just as God has a story to tell, so do you. You were put on this earth to make a difference; the vision within you is a spark of the divine fire. You carry inside you a central, organizing principle that enables you to construct a framework for accomplishing the vision God has placed in your heart.

As you seek to fulfill that vision, you've surrounded yourself with others who share that vision, that mission. You inspire each other to continue moving forward, even in times of uncertainty or opposition. As a leader, you're a careful, attentive listener, and you consistently solicit and focus on feedback of all types. You assess the context: the competitive environment, the obstacles you're likely to face, and the people, resources, strategies, and procedures you'll need to pursue your vision. You establish clarity within yourself around the mission, and you communicate to and solicit from others that same clarity. You use feedback to continually prove the accuracy of the communication you give and receive.

You build a team of people with diverse gifts, viewpoints, abilities, temperaments, and backgrounds because you know that the breakthrough you seek depends on creativity, intuitiveness, and relentless questioning of assumptions. This diverse team is united by a common purpose; it's aligned by the vision and by a focus on the long-term mission. That alignment, in turn, builds confidence up and down the team, as each member trusts the others to carry out their unique function in service of the mission.

As the leader of this diverse, yet aligned team, you model courage and conviction, even in the face of adversity, obstacles, and unforeseen challenges. You know you're leading the organization through uncharted territory, and you have confidence in your team's agility, resourcefulness, and ability to respond creatively to the unexpected.

You understand the difference between the urgent and the important, and you maintain your long-term vision, even amid the short-term distractions of day-to-day challenges. Your long-term focus allows you to balance urgency with vision, giving your team the confidence to respond to emergent challenges without losing sight of the strategic objectives.

Because of your long-term vision, you understand that failure, while not pleasant, is also not the end. Rather, it's an important teacher that can help you refine your methods, recalculate your course, and provide the important data points you need to find ultimate success. As a leader, you help your team learn from failure, realizing that it isn't a reflection on your leadership but is integral to the change process that always precedes breakthrough to challenging new frontiers.

You never forget that breakthroughs require looking at things differently than anyone else has, taking an untried approach. You accept that you'll need to go where others have never gone in order to find the new, the innovative. You also accept that because you are venturing into the unknown, you must help your organization balance the exhilaration of seeking the new opportunity with the fear of the untried and uncertain. You rely on the framework you've constructed in order to navigate the uncharted waters, believing that it gives you the tools you need to respond to the unexpected.

Beyond the Barriers

When Chuck Yeager broke the sound barrier in his Bell X-1 on October 14, 1947, no hard engineering data existed on the flight characteristics of an aircraft traveling at supersonic speeds.[22] Some thought it was possible that no aircraft could physically withstand the buffeting that would occur as it approached supersonic speed. Captain Yeager was literally flying into the unknown at more than 1,100 feet per second. And yet, once Yeager had accomplished this feat, his experience was soon duplicated many more times. By the 1950s, aircraft were routinely flying faster than the speed of sound, and by the 1970s, the Concorde was carrying passengers across the Atlantic at supersonic speeds.

Leaders with a well-constructed framework approach change with an attitude not only of acceptance, but anticipation.

Experienced pilots have a mantra: "Fly the airplane." What they mean by this is that no matter what happens during a flight, there are certain physical principles that govern an aircraft's behavior. The pilot's job is to engage those principles as effectively as possible, no matter what else is going on, until the aircraft is safely back on the ground. If you get into a patch of rough air, fly the airplane until things smooth out. If an engine cuts out, fly the airplane until you can find a place to land. If, like Captain "Sully" Sullenberger on US Airways Flight 1549 on January 15, 2009, you realize that your most viable safe landing spot is the Hudson River, you fly the airplane until you can bring it to rest on the surface of the river as safely as possible. You use the tools at your disposal to manage the unexpected. You do what you know to do for as long as you can do it until the situation becomes more controllable.

No doubt as Chuck Yeager strapped himself into the cockpit of the X-1 he was saying to himself, "Fly the airplane." Venturing into the untried and the unknown, he availed himself as much as possible of what he knew and what he could do.

It's much the same for leaders of organizations who are positioning themselves for a breakthrough. Like the first supersonic flight, breakthroughs always occur at the leading edge of knowledge and experience. Framework leadership provides a means to approach that leading edge with confidence and effectiveness. Leaders with a well-constructed framework approach change with an attitude not only of acceptance, but anticipation. They aren't foolhardy, but neither are they timid. They have a plan, and they execute it to energize and enable team members to respond as needed to changing conditions. They realize they can't know with certainty what lies ahead, but they understand that the only path to breakthrough lies through that uncertainty.

The Habit of the Extraordinary

I'm convinced that in order to remain relevant, leaders and organizations need to develop regular patterns of breakthrough behavior. Only by doing so can they produce the innovative results that will meet the rising challenges of the future.

Let's say the year is 1894, and you are the owner and director of Acme Buggy Whips, Inc. As the name of the company implies, everyone knows that you make the best buggy whips money can buy. Even your competitors in the buggy whip business know that no one can successfully compete with Acme for quality, workmanship, durability, or even pricing. You and your predecessors in the company have spent years developing the most efficient techniques, the best processes, and the highest standards in the buggy whip industry. You've got this whole thing down to an exact science. You've got the buggy whip market locked up tight.

Then, you read in your morning newspaper that a company in Germany, headed by one Karl Benz, has begun producing vehicles that are driven by a mechanical engine powered by the internal combustion of gasoline.[23] Of course, you know that people have been fooling around with such things since at least the early 1800s, when some Swiss engineer built a contraption that ran on hydrogen.[24] "It'll never catch on," you tell yourself, and you turn to the stock market reports on the next page.

A few years later, in 1908, you hear that Henry Ford, an engineer and manufacturer in Detroit, has begun mass-producing a vehicle called the Model T.[25] The newspapers are full of stories about the vehicle, and blacksmith shops all across the country—some of your best customers, in fact—are lining up to get approval to sell the machines to the public. Some are even learning how to repair them when they break down, which they often do. Despite this, more and more people are becoming automobile enthusiasts, even nagging their legislators for improvements to the local roads in order to accommodate the needs of the new vehicles.

You can see where this is going. Today, when we refer to an enterprise that's been overtaken by change to the point that it's no longer relevant, we refer to it as a "buggy-whip industry." The phrase has become synonymous with failure to innovate or to respond to evolving needs and trends.

As a leader, your most important task is to help your enterprise continue asking the What if questions. In order to remain engaged, effective, and relevant, you must consistently lead in a way that acknowledges and welcomes change and innovation. You must develop the habit of doing extraordinary things.

Regardless of what enterprise you are leading, from corporate to ministry, you can't afford for your organization to be left in the backwaters of change. You were put on this earth to make a difference, and in order to do that, you must continue to adapt, to change, to question assumptions, and to exercise the fundamentals of framework leadership. To paraphrase a TV show that was popular a few years ago, the next breakthrough is out there; you must cultivate the eyes to see it. Framework leadership will help you do that.

Becoming the Leader God Wants You to Be

There's nothing godly or inherently spiritual about irrelevance. In fact, I believe that God calls each one of us, in our own sphere of influence, to be intimately engaged and relevant as we live in this world. In order to be the salt and light Jesus describes in Matthew 5:13, we must be among people, taking our place in society, and offering the best that is within us.

Framework leadership enables you to carry out that mission. It gives you the skills, tools, and insights to bring your God-given passion to bear on the vision you've received.

There's a saying in ministry: "When God anoints, He enables." Another way of putting it is, "If God brings you to it; He'll bring you through it."

I believe that with all my heart. God has brought you to a unique time and place in the great, unfolding story He is writing, the story called Creation. But He hasn't just yanked you up and set you down in the middle of the script without also giving you what you need to play the part written for you.

Instead, God has placed within you a unique vision, a unique passion, and a unique ability to exercise both. His expectation is that you will allow free rein to the impulse to impact His world for good. His hand will guide you as you move through the process of change into the unknown, and His spirit will give you wisdom and

There's nothing godly or inherently spiritual about irrelevance.

perception as you listen to, seek alignment with, inspire, and enable others. The creative insights that lead to breakthroughs come through the work of God's Spirit within you; the courage and persistence to face and learn from failure come from the strength He gives. You are never going it alone.

I'm reminded of the words of the apostle Paul in his letter to the church at Corinth. As he informed them of his plans, he said, "I will stay on at Ephesus until Pentecost, because a great door for effective work has opened to me, *and there are many who oppose me*" (1 Corinthians 16:8–9, emphasis mine). What a revealing statement from this great and visionary leader of the church! Paul was at the epicenter of change in the early church, as faith in Christ moved from the solely Jewish audience of its earliest days into the broader Greco-Roman world. Paul led this change in his work of evangelization throughout the Mediterranean world.

And yet, as with any process of change, Paul encountered challenges and opposition. But significantly, he didn't allow this to change his view of what needed to be done. In fact, he announced his intention to stay right where he was—in the midst of his opponents—because he knew the importance of the work he had to do.

As you construct your own framework for leadership and engage with the vision God has given you, I hope you catch a glimpse of Paul's determination. I hope that when the inevitable trials and troubles come along, you will keep your eye on the long-term mission.

If you can do that, I'm confident you'll find the breakthrough you seek—taking you to new levels in your leadership destiny.

Journaling Your Own Breakthrough

One of the conversations I have consistently with members of the leadership team at Southeastern University concerns developing the habit of the disciplines necessary to continual assessment of the leadership framework. As we discussed in chapter 10, breakthrough behavior must involve a process of continual discovery, habitual questioning of assumptions, and a relentless unwillingness to rest on yesterday's successes. As I tell the team, "There is no 'rest' in breakthrough."

In order to cultivate the necessary behavioral habits, we've developed what we call Life/Time Management: a set of strategies that encourages awareness of personal disciplines, personal behaviors, and personal management in order to facilitate the mindset and awareness needed to continually revise the leadership framework. The following outline can serve as a journaling aid for you as you cultivate the behavioral and intellectual processes needed to evaluate your leadership framework.

Consider the prompt questions in the outline, or create your own questions, based on your individual experience. Then, journal your thoughts, reflections, and discoveries as you develop the habits of a breakthrough leader.

Your Breakthrough Framework

YEARLY WORDS TO DRIVE THE FRAMEWORK

Listening—missional discovery
- What am I hearing from my contacts (friends, clients, team members)?
- What themes are emerging?
- What are the implications for the operational environment?

Courage and conviction—missional determination to be different
- What are the opportunities in the environment?
- What would I attempt if there were no constraints?
- What do I need to know to develop an effective plan?

Intentional living—missional strategy
- What is the nature of this opportunity?
- How does this opportunity fit with God's design for my life?
- How does this opportunity engage my passion to make a difference?

Passion—contagious missional drive
- What do I care about most deeply?
- How can I communicate my passion most effectively?
- Which people in my environment share my passion?

Dream—missionally-driven innovation
- What resources do I need to make my vision a reality?
- What problems must be solved to move forward effectively?
- Is there a fresh or untried approach that I should consider?

BREAKTHROUGH THINKING (PERSONAL, "NEXT-LEVEL" LEADERSHIP)

Lifetime management (personal discipline awareness)
- How can I become more self-aware of my internal and external contexts?

Self-awareness (experiences, passions, people)
• How are the experiences, passions, and people in my life preparing me for the next opportunity?

Self-management (emotional, physical, mental, spiritual)
• How am I training myself to readiness for opportunity?

Opportunity awareness
• How can I prepare myself to perceive opportunities as they arise?

DISCERNMENT THINKING

Assessing my sphere of influence
• How can I improve my knowledge of the people in my framework?

"New Curve" direction
• How does my current level of success change my assumptions?

People around me
• Do I have the team I need to operate at my current or expected level of success?

Strategic Empowerment—Systems
• Are my current systems adequate for the level at which I expect to operate?

People
• Do I have the appropriate mix of talents/skills/passion to support the expected breakthrough?

Endnotes

1. Frederick Buechner, *Wishful Thinking: A Seeker's ABC* (New York: HarperOne, 1993), 118.

2. http://www.ted.com/talks/dan_phillips_creative_houses_ from_reclaimed_stuff.html (accessed November 30, 2015)

3. http://phoenixcommotion.com/media/ (accessed November 30, 2015)

4. http://www.people.com/people/archive/article/0,,201 36668,00 .html (accessed November 30, 2015)

5. Chapter epigraph as quoted in John Mack Faragher, *Daniel Boone: The Life and Legend of an American Pioneer* (New York: Holt, 1993), 65.

6. On results, as quoted in Frank Lewis Dyer and Thomas Commorford Martin, *Edison: His Life and Inventions* (New York: Harper & Brothers, 1910), accessed at Project Gutenberg, http://www.gutenberg.org/files/820/820-h/820-h.htm [accessed January 3, 2016]; on not giving up, as quoted in Deborah Hedstrom-Page, *From Telegraph to Light Bulb with Thomas Edison* (Nashville: B&H Publications, 2007), 22.

7. "*Portfolio*'s Worst American CEOs of All Time"; CNBC.com, April 30, 2009; retrieved August 25, 2014. Tony Mayo, "Context-Based Leadership"; *Harvard Business Review online*, July 24, 2007; https://hbr.org/2007/07/contextbased-leadership-1; retrieved December 6, 2015.

8. Quoted in Stephen Walsh, *Stravinsky: The Second Exile: France and America*, 1934–1971 (New York: Knopf, 2006).

9. Adapted from Gay Hendricks and Kathlyn Hendricks, *Attracting Genuine Love* (Boulder, CO: Sounds True, Inc., 2009), 67–68.

10. As quoted in Philip Sheldrake, *The Business of Influence: Reframing Marketing and PR for the Digital Age* (Chichester, UK: Wiley, 2011), 153.

11. Julie A. Oseid, "The Power of Clarity: Ulysses S. Grant as a Model of Writing 'So That There Could Be No Mistaking It.'" Association of Legal Writing Directors, Fall 2012 [online]; available at http://www.alwd.org/lcr/archives/fall-2012/oseid/ (accessed January 7, 2016).

12. As told in Roger Lohmann and Nancy Lohmann, *Social Administration* (New York: Columbia University Press, 2002), 350.

13. As reported in the *Denver Business Journal* [online], December 24, 2014; available at http://www.9news.com/story/ life/2014/12/24/what-a-nasa-janitor-can-teach-us-about-living-a-bigger-life/20859603/ (accessed January 8, 2016).

14. Mihaly Csikszentmihalyi, *Flow: The Psychology of Optimal Experience* (New York: Harper Perennial, 2008).

15. Thomas M. Hatfield, *Rudder: From Leader to Legend* (College Station: Texas A&M University Press, 2011).

16. Kathleen K. Reardon, "Courage as a Skill." *Harvard Business Review*, January 2007 [online]. Available at https://hbr. org/2007/01/courage-as-a-skill (accessed January 11, 2016).

17. Dwight D. Eisenhower, "Address at the Second Assembly of the World Council of Churches, Evanston, Illinois," August 19, 1954 [online]. Available at http://www.presidency.ucsb.edu/ ws/?pid=9991 (accessed January 18, 2016).

18. Stephen R. Covey, A. Roger Merrill, and Rebecca R. Merrill, *First Things First: To Live, to Love, to Learn, to Leave a Legacy* (New York: Simon and Schuster, 1994), 37.

19. Robert Goldman and Stephen Papson, *Nike Culture: The Sign of the Swoosh* (Thousand Oaks, CA: Sage Publications, 1998), 49.

20. Edward D. Hess, "Creating an Innovative Culture: Accepting Failure as Necessary." *Forbes*, June 20, 2012.

21. The Coverage, "'We Didn't Do Anything Wrong, but Somehow, We Lost,' Last Speech by Nokia's CEO," March 5, 2016 [online], available at http://thecoverage.my/stories/we-didnt-do-anything-wrong-but-somehow-we-lost-last-speech-by-nokias-ceo/ (accessed March 17, 2016).

22. John D. Anderson Jr., "Research in Supersonic Flight and the Breaking of the Sound Barrier." Available at http://history.nasa.gov/SP-4219/Chapter3.html (accessed January 23, 2016).

23. Daimler Group, "Company History," https://www.daimler.com/company/tradition/company-history/1885-1886.html (accessed January 24, 2016).

24. Erik Eckermann, *World History of the Automobile* (Warrendale, PA: Society of Automotive Engineers, 2001).

25. Ford Motor Company, "Model T Facts." https://media.ford.com/content/fordmedia/fna/us/en/news/2013/08/05/model-t-facts.html (accessed January 24, 2016).

About the Author

K ent Ingle is the president of Southeastern University. Previously, he served as the dean of the College of Ministry at Northwest University in Kirkland, Washington. He has also served eight years as a college professor and fifteen years as a pastor. Prior to entering professional ministry, Kent spent ten years as a television sports anchor for NBC and CBS. Kent holds an MTS from Vanguard University and a DMin from the Assemblies of God Theological Seminary. He is the author of *This Adventure Called Life* and *9 Disciplines of Enduring Leadership*. Kent and his wife, Karen, reside in Lakeland, Florida.

For More Information

Foreword by Jon Gordon
Wall Street Journal bestselling author of The Energy Bus and You Win in the Locker Room First

FRAMEWORK
LEADERSHIP

POSITION YOURSELF FOR TRANSFORMATIONAL CHANGE

KENT INGLE

Author of *This Adventure Called Life*
and *9 Disciplines of Enduring Leadership*

For more information about this and other valuable
resources visit *www.myhealthychurch.com*